MW01248933

Handbook of Investigation and Effective CAPA Systems

Handbook of Investigation and Effective CAPA Systems

Second Edition

José Rodríguez-Pérez

ASQ Quality Press
Milwaukee, Wisconsin

American Society for Quality, Quality Press, Milwaukee, WI 53203

Printed in the United States of America.

22 21 20 19 18 17 16 5 4 3 2

Library of Congress Cataloging-in-Publication Data

Rodríguez-Pérez, José, 1961–
Handbook of investigation and effective CAPA systems/
José Rodríguez-Pérez.
CAPA for the FDA-regulated industry.
Second Edition. | Milwaukee, WI: ASQ, 2016. | Revised Edition of the author's CAPA for the FDA-regulated industry, 2011. | Includes bibliographical references and index.
LCCN 2016005440 | ISBN 9780873899260 (hardcover : alk. paper)
LCSH: Pharmaceutical industry—Government policy—United States. | Food industry and trade—Government policy—United States. | Total Quality management—United States. | MESH: Drug Industry—organization & administration—United States. | Food Industry—organization & administration—United States. | Public Policy—United States. | Total Quality Management—United States. LCC HD9666.6 .R63 2016 | DDC 615.1068/1—dc23
LC record available at http://lccn.loc.gov/2016005440

Acquisitions Editor: Matt T. Meinholz
Project Editor: Paul Daniel O'Mara
Production Administrator: Randall Benson

ASQ Mission: The American Society for Quality advances individual, organizational, and community excellence worldwide through learning, quality improvement, and knowledge exchange.

Attention Bookstores, Wholesalers, Schools, and Corporations: ASQ Quality Press books, video, audio, and software are available at quantity discounts with bulk purchases for business, educational, or instructional use. For information, please contact ASQ Quality Press at 800-248-1946, or write to ASQ Quality Press, P.O. Box 3005, Milwaukee, WI 53201-3005.

To place orders or to request ASQ membership information, call 800-248-1946. Visit our Web site at www.asq.org/quality-press.

∞ Printed on acid-free paper

Quality Press
600 N. Plankinton Ave.
Milwaukee, WI 53203-2914
E-mail: authors@asq.org

The Global Voice of Quality™

Contents

List of Figures and Tables . . . . *ix*

Preface to the 2nd Edition . . . . *xi*

Acknowledgments . . . . *xiii*

Chapter 1 The Quality System and the Investigation and CAPA Element **1**

1.1. The Quality System and CAPA 1
1.2. Investigation and CAPA Relationship with Other Quality Subsystems 5
1.3. NCR or CAPA? Investigation Phase Versus Fixing Causes 7
1.4. Corrective or Preventive? 8

Chapter 2 Investigation and CAPA Requirements for the Life Sciences Regulated Industry **13**

2.1. FDA Pharmaceutical CGMP 14
2.2. FDA Medical Devices QSR 15
2.3. FDA Quality System Inspection Technique (QSIT) 17
2.4. FDA Guidance: Investigating Out-of-Specification (OOS) Test Results for Pharmaceutical Production 23
2.5. FDA Guidance: Quality Systems Approach to Pharmaceutical Current Good Manufacturing Practice Regulations 25
2.6. European Pharmaceutical GMP (*Eudralex* Volume 4) 27
2.7. Harmonization Processes: ICH and GHTF/IMDRF 29
2.8. ICH Q10: Pharmaceutical Quality System 30
2.9. ISO 13485 and the Non-U.S. Medical Devices Regulations 30

2.10. GHTF Quality Management System—Medical Devices—Guidance on Corrective Action and Preventive Action and Related QMS Processes 33
2.11. Complaint Investigations: Regulatory Expectations and Best Practices 33
2.12. Current Observations and Regulatory Trends for Investigations and CAPA system 35

Chapter 3 ISO 9001:2015—Nonconformance and CAPA requirements **39**

Chapter 4 Effective Investigations and CAPA Processes: From Problem Detection to Effectiveness Check **43**
4.1. Problem Detection: Discovering Problems 45
4.1.1. Sources of Data About Product and Quality Issues 45
4.1.2. Initial Impact Assessment 47
4.1.2.1. Risk Assessment 49
4.1.3. Process Trending 56
4.2. Problem Investigation: Discovering Root Causes 59
4.2.1. Symptoms, Causal Factors and Root Causes 60
4.2.2. Fixing Symptoms: Corrections 64
4.2.3. Problem Description 66
4.2.4. Barrier Analysis 70
4.2.5. Root Cause Identification Processes and Tools ... 72
4.2.5.1. The Investigation Plan 72
4.2.5.2. Root Cause Identification Tools 74
4.2.6. Root Cause Categories 77
4.3. CAPA Plan: Corrective and Preventive Actions to Fix Root Causes 80
4.3.1. Establish Effective Corrective and Preventive Actions 81
4.3.2. Validation and Verification Prior to Implementation 82
4.3.3. Implementation of Corrective and Preventive Actions 83
4.4. Effectiveness Evaluation 84
4.4.1. Verifying That Solutions Worked 84
4.4.2. Training Effectiveness 85

4.5. Management of the Investigation and CAPA System 90
4.5.1. Investigation and CAPA System Structure 90
4.5.2. Investigation and CAPA Process Metrics and U.S. FDA's Quality Metrics Program 91
4.5.3. Risk Management and the Investigation and CAPA System.......................... 94
4.5.3.1 CAPA System and FMEA................ 94
4.5.4. Management of External CAPA 96

Chapter 5 Human Error Investigation and Reduction 97
5.1. About Human Error 97
5.1.1. Data Integrity and Human Error 99
5.2. Human Error and Human Factor 100
5.3. Psychology and Classification of The Human Error 101
5.4. Human Factors 105
5.4.1. Compliance and Quality Culture............... 106
5.4.2. Workplace Involvement: Motivation and Attention.............................. 108
5.4.3. Adequate Supervision and Staffing............ 109
5.4.4. Procedures and Task Design.................. 110
5.4.5. Training and Performance.................... 115
5.4.6. Examples of Human Factors in Process Operations.......................... 116
5.5. How Organizations Deal with Human Errors? 118
5.6. Investigating Human Errors 119
5.7. Root Causes Related to Human Performance: My Own Findings Within The Regulated Industry 122
5.8. Human Errors and Retraining....................... 124
5.9. Working from Memory............................. 125
5.10. Multitasking and Human Errors 126
5.11. How to Reduce the Probability of Human Error 127

Chapter 6 Biggest Opportunities of The Investigation/CAPA System and How To Fix Them 133
6.1. Lack of Investigation Plan 133
6.2. Timeliness (Lack of) 134
6.3. Everything is an Isolated Event (Lack of Adequate Trending)........................ 138
6.4. Root Cause Not Identified 140
6.5. Root Causes Identified But Not Corrected 141
6.6. Correcting The Symptom Instead of the Cause 141
6.7. Lack of Interim Actions 142

6.8. Lack of True Preventive Actions 143
6.9. Lack of Effectiveness Verification of the Action Taken ... 144
6.10. Multiple CAPA Systems Without Correlation 146
6.11. Abuse of Human Error and Re-Training 147
6.12. Focusing More on the Software Than on the Investigation and CAPA System 147

Chapter 7 Developing an Internal Investigation and CAPA Expert Certification 149
7.1. Content of the Certification 149
7.2. Evaluating the Effectiveness of Investigation and CAPA Training Efforts 155

Chapter 8 Documenting Investigation and CAPA: Forms and Examples 157
8.1. Content of the Investigation Report 157
8.2. Content of the CAPA Plan 159
8.3. Compliance Writing 159
8.4. Forms 161
8.4.1. Investigation Report 162
8.4.2. Root Cause Analysis Checklist 164
8.4.3. Human Error Investigation 168
8.4.4. CAPA Plan 172
8.4.5. Investigation Report Assessment 173
8.4.6. CAPA Plan Assessment 177
8.5. Examples of Investigation Reports 179
8.6. CAPA Plan Examples 189
8.7. Final Recommendations 194

Appendix A 197
Additional Resources 197
Useful Web Pages 197

Acronyms *199*

Glossary *201*

Bibliography *207*

Index *211*

List of Figures and Tables

Figure 1.1	The Investigation and CAPA system and the manufacturing quality system	5
Table 1.1	Quality data sources within the QMS	6
Table 1.2	Investigation and CAPA sources	6
Figure 1.2	Feeders of the Investigation and CAPA System	7
Table 1.3	CAPA History	9
Table 1.4	Corrective or preventive?	11
Figure 4.1	The Investigation and CAPA process flow	43
Figure 4.2	The Investigation and CAPA system	44
Figure 4.3	The ineffective Investigation and CAPA circle	45
Figure 4.4	Relationship among 820.90, 820.100, and 820.198	46
Table 4.1	Risk assessment criteria	50
Table 4.2	Risk assessment score matrix	53
Table 4.3	Example of risk assessment	54
Figure 4.5	Risk prioritization of investigations	55
Table 4.4	Type of nonconformance investigations	56
Figure 4.6	Scrap monthly rates	60
Figure 4.7	Root cause elements	61
Figure 4.8	Investigation and CAPA example	63
Table 4.5	Symptoms, causal factors and root causes	63
Table 4.6	Examples of causal factors and root causes	64
Table 4.7	Symptoms and corrections	65
Table 4.8	Typical laboratory error investigation	66
Figure 4.9	Timeline of event	69
Figure 4.10	Change analysis graph	69
Table 4.9	Barrier controls	71
Table 4.10	Barrier control analysis example	71
Figure 4.11	Fault tree analysis example	76
Table 4.12	The four levels of Kirkpatrick Model	87
Figure 4.12	Interaction between FMEA and CAPA	95

Figure 5.1	Types of human errors	101
Table 5.1	Slips and lapses of memory	102
Figure 5.2	Human factor domains	106
Table 5.2	Comparison between human and machine capabilities	117
Table 5.3	Human error investigation and prevention DOs and DON'Ts	130
Figure 6.1	The Weibull distribution or bathtub curve	137
Table 7.1	Investigation and CAPA expert certification (Day 1)	150
Table 7.2	Investigation and CAPA expert certification (Day 2)	151
Table 7.3	Investigation and CAPA expert certification (Day 3)	152
Table 7.4	Investigation and CAPA expert certification (Day 4)	153
Table 7.5	Investigation and CAPA expert certification (Day 5)	154
Table 7.6	Investigation and CAPA expert certification evaluation levels	155
Table 8.1	Compliance writing DOs and DON'Ts	160
Table 8.2	Investigation report	162
Table 8.3	Root cause analysis checklist	164
Table 8.4	Human error investigation	168
Table 8.5	CAPA plan	172
Table 8.6	Investigation report assessment	173
Table 8.7	CAPA plan assessment	177
Table 8.8	Final Investigation and CAPA recommendations	194

Preface to the 2nd Edition

The new title of this second edition reflects the importance of the investigation/root cause analysis stage as the necessary preceding step of any effective corrective and preventive action system. This title also echoes the fact that investigation and CAPA are concepts used in many sectors besides the FDA regulated industry, such as: automotive, electronics, aerospace, telecommunications, process industry, and so on. It is the hope that this book will reach those persons in other industries and become an essential reference for them. Finally, the Merriam-Webster's Collegiate Dictionary defines handbook as "a concise reference book covering a particular subject", which is a perfect match for the intention of this book.

Chapter 1 has been enhanced with updated information about the importance of the CAPA system within the quality system for the medical products regulated industry. The regulatory impact of a deficient investigation and CAPA system is paramount and it is one of the few major regulatory issues applying to all type of regulated products. Manufacturers of human drug, medical devices, food, veterinary, and biologic products share the same kind of problems and opportunities for their investigation and CAPA systems.

Chapter 2 was updated with current versions of regulations (U.S. FDA, EU, ISO 13485, and so on) and a new section (Chapter 2.11) was added to cover the regulatory expectation of customer complaint investigations. Deficiencies related to this specific topic are being increasingly included in regulatory reports by U.S. FDA as well as by international inspectors.

Chapter 3 covers investigation and CAPA elements of the 2015 revision of ISO 9001.

Chapter 4 covers the complete investigation and CAPA cycle, from problem detection to monitoring of CAPA effectiveness. New sections were added covering the investigation plan and the new U.S. FDA quality metric guidance. Also, a section discusses the tight relationship between CAPAs and FMEA.

Chapter 5 is completely new and fully devoted to human errors and human factors and their impact on the investigation and CAPA system. A new investigation form has been developed containing 50 items to be considered during any human error investigation.

Chapter 6 describes a dozen of the most common pitfalls usually encountered in the investigation and CAPA world of regulated companies.

Chapter 7 includes an example of an investigation and CAPA expert certification program being used for many companies. It contains the elements of the certification in the form of a detailed syllabus and also the elements that can be include to measure the effectiveness of that training effort.

Chapter 8 contains forms and examples of the different elements (investigation report, root causes checklist, human error investigation, CAPA plan, and so on) covered in this book. Fully usable forms are included in the companion CD in Microsoft Word format.

Acknowledgments

To the many readers of the first edition who shared with me their comments and praises. Your comments always made my day!

A special thanks to my friend and colleague Manuel Peña who, along with me, is traveling around the world teaching the principles of this book as part of the Investigation and CAPA Expert Certification.

And finally, but not the least important, a gigantic thanks to my family for their continuous support. My short career as a writer has only been possible thanks to your support.

1

The Quality System and the Investigation and CAPA Element

1.1 THE QUALITY SYSTEM AND CAPA

A quality system is a set of formalized business practices that define management responsibilities for organizational structure, processes, procedures, and resources needed to fulfill product or service requirements, customer satisfaction, and continuous improvement. A quality management system (QMS) is a set of interrelated elements (processes) used to direct and control an organization with regard to quality. In other words, a quality system dictates how quality policies are implemented and quality objectives are achieved.

Continuous improvement is the result of ongoing activities to evaluate and enhance products, processes, and the entire quality system to increase their efficiency and effectiveness. The organization must continuously improve its QMS through the use of its quality policy, quality objectives, audit results, analysis of data, corrective and preventive actions, and the management review processes.

Analyzing data is an essential activity for any possible improvement at any level (system, process, and product/service). The organization must collect and analyze appropriate data to demonstrate the suitability and effectiveness of the QMS. This must include data generated as a result of monitoring and measurement as well as data gathered from other relevant sources. The analysis of data will provide information on customer satisfaction, conformity to product or service requirements, trends of processes and products including opportunities for preventive action, and suppliers.

Corrective action is one of the most important improvement activities. It seeks to permanently eliminate the causes of problems that have a negative impact on systems, processes, and products. Corrective action involves finding the causes of some specific problem and then implementing the necessary actions to avoid a reoccurrence. Preventive actions are aimed at preventing the occurrence of potential problems. Corrections are the third basic element of the corrective and preventive action system (CAPA). Corrections address the symptoms rather than the causes and sometimes are referred to as immediate, remedial, or containment actions. The concept of CAPA is not restricted to any particular industry or sector. It is a widely-accepted concept, basic to any quality management system. Since quality systems strive to continuously improve systems, processes, and products/services, there must be mechanisms in place to recognize existing or potential quality issues, take the appropriate steps necessary to investigate and resolve those issues, and, finally, make sure the same issues do not recur. Processes of the life sciences regulated industries (the manufacturing of medical devices, biopharmaceuticals, and traditional drugs) are plagued with deviations and nonconformities.

Worldwide regulatory agencies perform thousands of inspections every year. Too often investigation and CAPA system violations are at the top of the list.

Within the United States, lack of adequate investigations, lack of true root cause analysis, lack of effective corrective actions, and lack of true preventive actions are common findings pointed out by Food and Drug Administration's (FDA) inspectors. As evidenced by the significant number of problems related to this issue, companies are facing many challenges in making the investigation and CAPA system work as intended. Life sciences regulated companies must ensure their investigation and CAPA system looks beyond product issues and considers other quality issues including problems associated with processes and systems. Unfortunately, a significant number of regulated companies are approaching the investigation and CAPA system very lightly, implementing corrections but no corrective and preventive actions.

Investigation and CAPA systems are inherently data driven. Without adequate and relevant data, it can be difficult to draw definitive conclusions about systems, processes, or product quality issues. One of the challenges many companies face is the proliferation of uncorrelated data repository systems within the organization. A typical example for U.S. companies is the existence of two separate systems (domestic and foreign) for investigating customer complaints. Another example is the lack of relationship between supplier and internal CAPA systems. By having a unified investigation and CAPA system, a company will be better able to diagnose the health of its quality system and will have a better chance of recognizing and resolving important quality issues.

As the quality system within an organization matures, there should be a natural shift in emphasis from corrective action to preventive action. Issues that must be corrected usually become obvious. However, issues that have the potential for becoming a problem are less readily recognized. How can a firm examine its internal data to find those few situations that might be the precursors of problems down the road? The answer is part of the regulations. Companies must establish methods to evaluate both the *nonconformance* data (which will feed the corrective action portion of the system) and the *in-conformance* data (which will be the basis for preventive actions).

An effective investigation and CAPA system must be a *closed loop* system. This term refers to at least two elements of the system. First, it means there are sufficient controls in place to ensure the investigations and CAPA process run through all the required steps to completion, and that management and those responsible for quality have visibility and input to the process. In addition, top management must review the outputs of the investigations and CAPA system. Very often companies focus on completing the individual tasks of a particular corrective action, yet lose track of the original purpose of the investigations and CAPA system. For example, a particular product problem may be resolved, but no evaluation is ever performed to ensure the solution was effective. In this example, the loop was never closed.

Second, an effective investigation and CAPA system closes the loop on many of the documented issues by directly providing input into basic elements of the QMS such as design control. For example, nonconforming product procedures are directed at assuring that the nonconforming product is identified and corrected prior to distribution or prevented from being distributed. Frequently, a correction or temporary change will be implemented to assure that the affected material is fixed. An effective investigation and CAPA system will require the problem to be investigated and its root causes effectively addressed with the appropriate corrective actions.

A documented procedure for the investigation and CAPA system must define requirements for the following elements:

1. Collect and analyze quality data to identify existing and potential causes of nonconforming products or other quality problems.
2. Investigate the causes of existing and potential nonconformities.
3. Identify corrective and preventive actions.
4. Verify or validate corrective and preventive action prior to implementation.
5. Implement corrective and preventive actions.
6. Evaluate the effectiveness of implemented corrective and preventive actions.

7. Ensure that the information related to quality problems or nonconforming products is disseminated to those directly responsible for assuring the quality of such product or the prevention of such problems.
8. Submit relevant information on identified quality problems, as well as corrective and preventive actions, for management review.

Finally, all investigation and CAPA system activities, and all quality system activities in general, must follow a risk-based approach. Because all existing and potential problems do not have the same significance and criticality, the prioritization of such actions must correlate with the risk and the magnitude of each situation.

The four key CAPA definitions are:

- **CAPA (corrective action and preventive action):** A systematic approach that includes actions needed to correct (correction), avoid recurrence (corrective action), and eliminate the cause of potential nonconforming product and other quality problems (preventive action).
- **Correction**: Action to eliminate a detected nonconformity. Corrections typically are one-time fixes. A correction is an immediate solution such as repair or rework. Corrections are also known as remedial or containment action.
- **Corrective action:** Action to eliminate the causes of an *existing* (detected) nonconformity or other undesirable situation. The corrective action should eliminate the *recurrence* of the root cause(s).
- **Preventive action:** Action to eliminate the causes of a *potential* nonconformity or other undesirable potential situation. Preventive action should prevent the *occurrence* of the potential issue by eliminating the occurrence of the root cause(s).

In summary, the purpose of the investigation and CAPA system is trifold:

a. Collect and analyze product, process, and system information based on appropriate statistical methodology to detect existing and potential quality system problems.
b. Investigate the cause(s) of significant (based on risk) existing and potential product and quality problems.
c. Take appropriate, effective, and comprehensive actions.

1.2 INVESTIGATION AND CAPA RELATIONSHIP WITH OTHER QUALITY SUBSYSTEMS

The investigation and CAPA system are critical components of an effective QMS and they must maintain a close relationship with other quality subsystems (as depicted in Figure 1.1). The ultimate goal of any regulated company must be to have an investigation and CAPA system that is compliant, effective, and efficient. All relevant subsystems that may produce nonconformances must be part of the process. The investigation and CAPA system relates to many others quality data sources within a QMS as depicted in Table 1.1.

There are multiple feeders to the investigation and CAPA system, both internal and external to the company (as represented in Figure 1.2). Internal processes encompass both *nonconformance* and *in-conformance* results, internal audits and assessments, management reviews, and so on. External sources of CAPA process inputs are supplier audits and assessments, customer feedback, and results from external audits and assessment such as regulatory agencies, ISO, and so on as depicted in Table 1.2. A detailed discussion of those feeders can be found in Chapter 4.1.1.

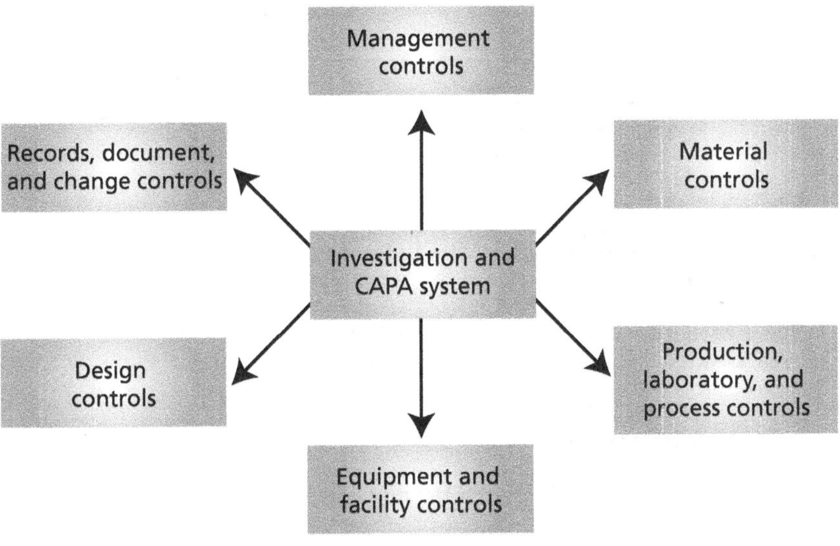

Figure 1.1 The Investigation and CAPA system and the manufacturing quality system.

Table 1.1 Quality data sources within the QMS.

Quality Data Sources within the QMS
Nonconforming products Complaints Investigations Process validations Document changes Calibration and preventive maintenance Purchasing/Supplier programs Audits (internal, third party, regulatory inspections, and so on) Management reviews Medical device reports (MDR) Field alert reports (FAR) Recalls and field actions Laboratory investigations Design changes/product reformulations Testing (incoming, in-process, finished product and stability) Product returns Service and installation

Table 1.2 Investigation and CAPA sources.

Internal Sources	External Sources
Nonconforming reports Laboratory failures Equipment data (calibration, preventive maintenance, and repair) Scrap/yield data Rework data Returned product Internal audits Process control data Acceptance activities (incoming, in-process, finished product, and stability)	Complaints Field service reports Legal claim External audits FDA's MDRs FDA's FARs Scientific literature Social media

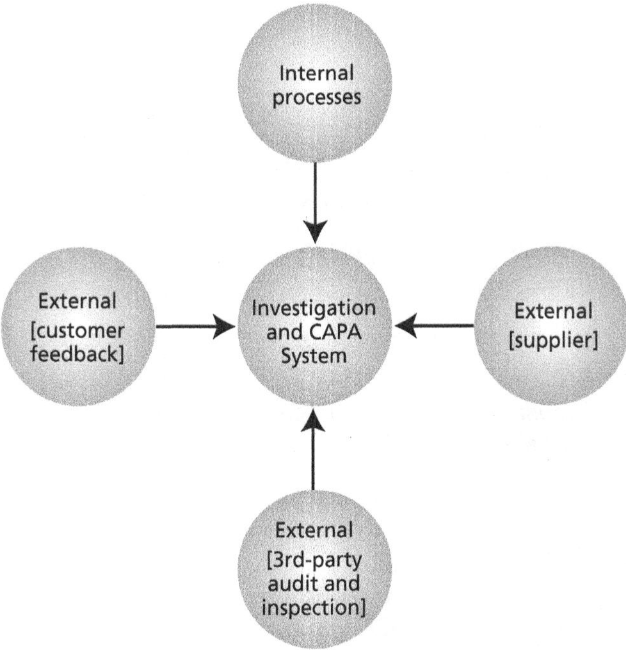

Figure 1.2 Feeders of the Investigation and CAPA system.

1.3 NCR OR CAPA? INVESTIGATION PHASE VERSUS FIXING CAUSES

A lot of confusion and lack of uniformity exist in many organizations when referring to what is a nonconformance report (NCR) and what should be part of a CAPA report. To complicate things even more, there is a notable lack of understanding of the meaning of CAPA within the industry. In this chapter we will try to clarify the first element, while we will elaborate on the explanation of the differences between corrective and preventive in the next chapter.

The CAPA system takes care of implementing corrective actions, and preventive actions resulting from the investigation of complaints, product rejections, nonconformances, recalls, deviations, audits, regulatory inspections and findings, and trends from process performance and product quality monitoring as established in ICH Q10.[1]

[1] ICH Q10 Pharmaceutical Quality System

Therefore we can clearly divide the CAPA system into the following two elements:

1. A structured *investigation process* approach to be used with the objective of determining the root causes. The level of effort, formality, and documentation of the investigation should be commensurate with the level of risk.
2. The implementation of *appropriate actions* covering:
   a. the remedial corrections of an identified problem
   b. corrective actions to avoid reoccurrences of the root cause(s)
   c. preventive actions to prevent the (first time) occurrence of the cause of a potential nonconformity or other undesirable potential situation

The investigation phase can undergo under many different names, such as complaint investigation, nonconformance investigation, deviation investigation, out-of-specification investigation, and so on. Complaints, laboratory failures (OOS), and nonconformances are only *symptoms*, and the objective of these investigations is to understand the problem and to find the root cause(s) that creates this symptom. The investigation phase (under whatever name we may use for it) must be focused on discovering the root cause(s) associated with this event. Chapter 4.1 and 4.2 cover extensively the investigational phase of the CAPA system.

On the other hand, we typically refer to CAPA documents as the forms used to document actions (correction, corrective action, and/or preventive actions) including the CAPA Plan. Chapter 4.3 and 4.4 describe this part of the CAPA system.

However, there are companies that use the term CAPA to identify high-level investigations as well. In other words, they use CAPA to investigate big nonconformities or high-risk situations. For this reason, one of the first things I do when I meet with managers to discuss CAPA is to ask them to define CAPA.

We recommend using the investigation form to document the investigational process and using the CAPA form to document the action taken to fix those root causes encountered during the investigational phase.

1.4 CORRECTIVE OR PREVENTIVE?

One of the most sterile debates anyone can witness is the discussion between CAPA professionals about whether a specific action they are working on should be considered corrective or preventive. The debate is pointless because what really matters is whether the action would address a root cause.

To add even more confusion, just read the formal definition of corrective action. ASQ/ANSI/ISO 9000:2015 defines corrective action as "action to eliminate the cause of a nonconformity and to prevent recurrence." ANSI/AAMI/ISO 13485-2003 contains the same definition, and the FDA regulation for medical devices (Title 21 CFR §820.100) establishes that each manufacturer shall identify "the action(s) needed to correct and *prevent* recurrence of nonconforming product and other quality problems." They use the word *prevent* as part of the *corrective action* definition. Chapter 3 discusses the use and interpretation of those concepts in the new ISO 9001:2015 standard.

A similar lack of clarity can be found in the 2006 FDA's Guidance for Industry Quality System Approach to Pharmaceutical GMP, which adequately describes corrective action as a reactive element aimed to potentially prevent recurrence of a similar problem while it describes preventive action as the action taken to avert recurrence of a similar potential problem. Table 1.3[2] describes the historical relation between corrective action and preventive action.

Table 1.3 CAPA history.

Standard	Content
1963—MIL-Q-9858A Quality program requirements	Corrective and preventive concepts placed under the same section
1970—10 CFR 50	Part 16 of the nuclear power generation federal regulation covered corrective action principles. No mention to preventive actions.
1987—ISO 9001—Quality management system	The first edition of the ISO 9001 standard included as clause 16 the requirement of procedures for investigating the cause of nonconforming product and corrective action need to prevent recurrence. No explicit mention to preventive actions.
1994—ISO 9001—Quality management system	The second edition of ISO 9001 separated the concept of corrective action and preventive action

(Continued)

[2] Modified from Arter, D. (2015)

(Continued)

Table 1.3 CAPA history.

Standard	Content
1997—U.S. FDA 21 CFR 820	Under subpart J introduced the concept of corrective and preventive action without a clear definition or separation of both concepts. It states: "identifying the action(s) needed to correct and prevent recurrence."
1999—U.S. FDA Quality System Inspection Technique guide	The QSIT guide defines corrective action as the "action taken to address an existing product or quality problem." It also states that it "should include action to correct the existing product nonconformity or quality problems and to prevent the recurrence of the problem."
2000—ISO 9001—Quality management system	Clauses 8.5.2 (corrective action) and 8.5.3 (preventive action) were maintained essentially identical to the 1994 definitions. No changes were made in the ISO 9001:2008 update.
2006—U.S. FDA's Guidance to Industry Quality System approach to pharmaceutical cGMP regulations	In this document, the FDA tries to separate both concepts but they didn't select the best wording to describe preventive action: "action to avert recurrence of a similar potential problem." Only the inclusion of "potential" helps to understand the concept of preventive.
2015—ISO 9001—Quality management system	One of the key purposes of implementing a QMS is to act as a preventive tool. As a result, the formal requirement related to preventive action was removed in the 2015 version and replaced with the risk-based thinking. As a result, the corrective action clause has been replaced by a new clause named "Nonconformity and corrective action" (10.2) while the preventive action clause has been deleted and its spirit has been incorporated as part of a new clause (6.1) named "Actions to address risks and opportunities."

To avoid any confusion, the word *prevent* is replaced by the word *eliminate* throughout this book; the definition of *corrective action* will read "action to eliminate the causes an *existing* (detected) nonconformity or other undesirable situation. The corrective action should eliminate the recurrence of the root cause(s)."

A second common source of confusion and misunderstanding is deeper and more philosophical. Let's say that company A has a situation where root cause Z is creating a potentially dangerous upward trend, but the result is still within specification. Someone can argue that because the result is still *in-conformance,* the action to be taken can be categorized as preventive. Others may argue that it is a corrective action because the cause was already acting, although the final result is still in-conformance. My opinion is that it is a preventive action, but whatever name you choose (corrective or preventive) is fine because the action addresses a root cause not a symptom; the important issue is to implement the action as soon as possible.

For clarification purposes, Table 1.4 contains the rules followed in this book.

Table 1.4 Corrective or preventive?

Situation	Examples
Name it *corrective action* only if you already have a product nonconformance or process noncompliance	• Product failing specifications • Confirmed customer complaint • Use of obsolete or non-approved documents • Audit finding of product nonconformance or process noncompliance
Name it *preventive action* whenever the product, process, or system is still in conformance, but you discover root causes with the potential to create nonconformities	• Developing adverse trends from a monitoring system (run chart or control chart) – Shifts – Trends – High variability, and so on
Name it *preventive action* if it is purely a recommendation to enhance or improve any product, process, or system	• Changing to new material or new design • Implementing new (enhanced) processes

A typical situation that occurs during nonconformance investigations is the simultaneous discovery of both existing and potential root causes. In those cases, actions taken to eliminate the causes of an existing nonconformance will be *corrective* actions, while actions taken to eliminate identified potential causes will be considered *preventive* actions. It is possible to have both categories of actions within the same CAPA plan.

A third controversy occurs when the same action can be considered both corrective and preventive when applied to different situations. Some CAPA professionals believe that once you have a corrective action (because you already had a nonconformance) to whatever product, process, or system you extend it, it will always be a corrective action. Other professionals, including myself, believe that if the same action can be extended to other products/processes/systems *not yet affected by this root cause,* then it should be considered a preventive action.

Chapter 3 covers nonconformances and CAPA system requirements for the new ISO 9001:2015 with a discussion related to the elimination of the term *preventive action* from this new version.

2

Investigation and CAPA Requirements for the Life Sciences Regulated Industry

This chapter details those requirements for the investigation and CAPA system found in several U.S. and international life science regulations, as well as in the international standard ISO 13485, which applies to medical device manufacturers.

In the U.S., the main sources of investigation and CAPA regulations are the current good manufacturing practices (CGMP) for finished drugs (Title 21 CFR §210 & 211) and the medical devices quality system requirements (QSR) contained in Title 21 CFR §820. Several guidelines and guidances[1] from the FDA will be reviewed in this chapter. It is important to note that U.S. FDA regulations are generally considered to be the most comprehensive of all medical product regulations; many non-U.S. regulations are derived from FDA requirements.

In the European Union (EU), pharmaceutical good manufacturing practices are included in volume 4 of the *EudraLex* (the rules governing medicinal products in the EU). It contains guidance for the interpretation of the principles and guidelines of CGMP for medicinal products for human and veterinary use laid down in Commission Directive 91/356/EEC, as amended by Directive 2003/94/EC and 91/412/EEC respectively. In the case of medical devices, the market is divided into three areas for regulatory purposes:

a. Active Implantable Medical Devices Directive 90/385 EEC (AIMD)

b. Medical Device Directive 93/42 EEC (MDD), and

c. In Vitro Diagnostic Directive 79/98 EC (IVDD).

[1] FDA guidance documents do not establish legally enforceable responsibilities. Instead, guidances describe the Agency's current thinking on a topic and should be viewed only as recommendations unless specific regulatory or statutory requirements are cited. The use of the word *should* in Agency guidances means that something is suggested or recommended, but not required. Author's comments: It is wise to follow the FDA current thinking.

These three directives must be considered a set because the AIMD was amended by the MDD and the IVDD amended the MDD.

Topics within this chapter are divided between U.S. and non-U.S. regulations. Within each, regulations are ordered by date of implementation. Following is an outline of this chapter's organization:

- FDA Pharmaceutical CGMP (Title 21 CFR §210 & 211)
- FDA Medical Devices QSR (Title 21 CFR §820)
- FDA Quality System Inspection Technique (QSIT)
- FDA Investigation Out-of-Specification (OOS) Guidance
- FDA Quality Systems Approach to Pharmaceutical Current Good Manufacturing Practice Regulations Guidance
- European Pharmaceutical GMP (*EudraLex* volume 4)
- Harmonization Processes: ICH and GHTF/IMDRF
- ICH Q10 Pharmaceutical Quality System
- ISO 13485 and the Non-U.S. Medical Devices Regulations
- Global Harmonization Task Force—Quality Management System—Medical Devices—Guidance on corrective action and preventive action and related QMS processes
- Current Regulatory Trends for investigation and CAPA system

2.1 FDA PHARMACEUTICAL CGMP

The U.S. regulations governing drugs can be found in the Title *21* of the *Code of Federal Regulations*. Parts 210 and 211 are named respectively *Current Manufacturing Practice in Manufacturing, Processing, Packing, or Holding of Drugs* And *Current Manufacturing Practice for Finished Pharmaceuticals*. Originally issued in 1971, they experienced major revisions during 1978 and 1995. Sections related to investigation of unwanted situations can be found throughout the regulations. The CAPA acronym was first adopted by the FDA during the development of the medical device quality system regulations in the 1990s.

§211.22 Responsibilities of quality control unit

"There shall be a quality control unit...and the authority to review production records to assure that no errors have occurred or, if errors have occurred, that they have been fully investigated."

§211.100 Written procedures; deviations

"Written production and process control procedures shall be followed.... Any deviation from the written procedures shall be recorded and justified."

§211.160 General requirements (Laboratory Controls)

"Any deviation from the written specifications, standards, sampling plans, test procedures, or other laboratory control mechanisms shall be recorded and justified."

§211.192 Production record review

"All drug product production and control records, including those for packaging and labeling, shall be reviewed and approved by the quality control unit to determine compliance with all established, approved written procedures before a batch is released or distributed. Any unexplained discrepancy (including a percentage of theoretical yield exceeding the maximum or minimum percentages established in master production and control records) or the failure of a batch or any of its components to meet any of its specifications shall be thoroughly investigated, whether or not the batch has already been distributed. The investigation shall extend to other batches of the same drug product and other drug products that may have been associated with the specific failure or discrepancy. A written record of the investigation shall be made and shall include the conclusions and follow-up."

United States v Barr Laboratories, Inc. 1993

This was a landmark decision because it provided legal strength to the concept "you cannot test a product into compliance." It also established some requirements for failure investigation additional to those already included in CGMP. Among them:

- Specifies content of failure report
- Requires listing and evaluation of lots potentially affected
- Specifies that elements of "thoroughness" vary depending on nature and impact of the event
- Establishes that all investigations must be performed promptly, within thirty business days of the problem's occurrence, and recorded in written investigation or failure reports

2.2 FDA MEDICAL DEVICES QSR

The FDA published its *Medical Devices: Current Good Manufacturing Practice (CGMP) Final Rule: Quality System Regulations (QSR)* in October 1996 and it became effective June 1, 1997. This publication changed the focus of the regulatory agency to a "beyond compliance" approach. The various elements of the quality system (subsystems) are interconnected and interdependent. Companies must develop a systematic approach to their processes in order to be able to produce quality goods. Three main areas distinguish this new regulation from the typical CGMP used for drugs:

- Design and development focus
- Purchasing control affecting suppliers, contractors, and consultants
- Corrective and preventive actions subsystem

Three subparts of the QSR are directly related to investigation and corrective and preventive actions:

- Subpart I §820.90 Nonconforming product
- Subpart J §820.100 Corrective and Preventive Action
- Subpart M §820.198 Records (Complaint files)

§820.90(a) Control of nonconforming product establishes that:

"Each manufacturer shall establish and maintain procedures to control product that does not conform to specified requirements. The procedures shall address the identification, documentation, evaluation, segregation, and disposition of nonconforming product. The evaluation of nonconformance shall include a determination of the need for an investigation and notification of the persons or organizations responsible for the nonconformance. The evaluation and any investigation shall be documented."

The distribution and justification for concessions (allowance to use otherwise nonconforming product, often done through a Material Review Board) must be documented and based on scientific evidence. Concessions should be closely monitored and not become normal practice. Deficiencies would include a lack of scientific evidence for justification of the concession. If a concession resulted in a change of product specifications (form, fit or function), the change should be evaluated for possible risk-based regulatory impact.

The CAPA subsystem is described in Subpart J. §820.100:

a. "Each manufacturer shall establish and maintain procedures for implementing corrective and preventive action. The procedures shall include requirements for:

1. Analyzing processes, work operations, concessions, quality audit reports, quality records, service records, complaints, returned product, and other sources of quality data to identify existing and potential causes of nonconforming product, or

other quality problems. Appropriate statistical methodology shall be employed where necessary to detect recurring quality problems;

2. Investigating the cause of nonconformities relating to product, processes, and the quality system;
3. Identifying the action(s) needed to correct and prevent recurrence of nonconforming product and other quality problems;
4. Verifying or validating the corrective and preventive action to ensure that such action is effective and does not adversely affect the finished device;
5. Implementing and recording changes in methods and procedures needed to correct and prevent identified quality problems;
6. Ensuring that information related to quality problems or nonconforming product is disseminated to those directly responsible for assuring the quality of such product or the prevention of such problems; and
7. Submitting relevant information on identified quality problems, as well as corrective and preventive actions, for management review.

b. All activities required under this section, and their results, shall be documented."

2.3 FDA QUALITY SYSTEM INSPECTION TECHNIQUE (QSIT)

Once the QSR were issued in 1996, the FDA created a team to reengineer the inspection process used by the Agency to perform quality system/good manufacturing practices inspections at medical device manufacturing facilities. The new inspection technique was called the Quality System Inspection Technique (QSIT). The QSIT approach to inspections was derived from the theory that there are seven subsystems in the QSR (21 CFR §820). Four primary areas were chosen to focus the inspection: management controls, design controls, corrective and preventive actions (CAPA), and production and process controls. The remaining three subsystems are covered via "linkages" within the QSIT guide.

Satellite programs are included in the QSIT inspection due to their correlation in the inspection process with the related subsystem. The CAPA subsystem is the logical "jumping-off" point to begin inspecting for medical device reporting, corrections and removals, and medical device tacking programs that relate to a firm's post-market activities.

Rather than evaluating every aspect of the firm's quality system, the so-called "top-down" subsystem approach focuses on those elements that are most important in meeting the requirements of the quality system regulation and that are key quality indicators. Between 6 and 15 inspectional objectives are provided for the review of each subsystem. The review includes both a (broad) review of whether the firm has procedures in place and appears to meet the requirements, and a closer (detailed) review of some records to verify that the requirements have been implemented in actual production, design, and daily quality assurance situations. Without a doubt, this FDA document provides an extraordinary benchmark, advising companies about where to align internal audit programs. The QSIT describes the CAPA subsystem as one of the most important quality system elements with an equally important purpose:

> To collect information, analyze information, identify and investigate product and quality problems, and take appropriate and effective corrective and/or preventive action to prevent their recurrence. Verifying or validating corrective and preventive actions, communicating corrective and preventive action activities to responsible people, providing relevant information for management review, and documenting these activities are essential in dealing effectively with product and quality problems, preventing their recurrence, and preventing or minimizing device failures.

I strongly recommend that anyone involved in CAPA read and fully understand the ten inspectional objectives. This is the most detailed information about the CAPA subsystem the FDA has ever provided:

1. *Verify that CAPA system procedures that address the requirements of the quality system regulation have been defined and documented.*

Review the firm's corrective and preventive action procedure. If necessary, have management provide definitions and interpretation of words or terms such as *nonconforming product, quality audit, correction, prevention, timely,* and others. It is important to gain a working knowledge of the firm's corrective and preventive action procedure before beginning the evaluation of this subsystem.

NOTE: Corrective action taken to address an existing product or quality problem should include action to correct the existing product nonconformity or quality problems and prevent the recurrence of the problem.

The CAPA procedure should include procedures regarding how the firm will meet the requirements for all elements of the CAPA subsystem. All procedures should have been implemented. Once you have gained knowledge of the firm's corrective and preventive action procedure, begin with determining whether the firm has a system for the identification and input of quality data into the CAPA subsystem. Such data includes information regarding product and quality problems (and potential problems) that may require corrective and/or preventive action.

2. *Determine whether appropriate sources of product and quality problems have been identified. Confirm that data from these sources are analyzed to identify existing product and quality problems that may require corrective action.*

The firm should have methods and procedures to input product or quality problems into the CAPA subsystem. Product and quality problems should be analyzed to identify those that may require corrective action.

The firm should routinely analyze data regarding product and quality problems. This analysis should include data and information from all acceptance activities, complaints, service records, and returned product records. The firm must capture and analyze data from acceptance activities relating to component, in-process, and finished device testing. Information obtained subsequent to distribution should also be captured and analyzed. This includes complaints, service activities, and returned products as well as information relating to concessions (quality and nonconforming products), quality records, and other sources of quality data. Examples of other sources of quality data include quality audits, installation reports, lawsuits, and so on.

3. *Determine whether sources of product and quality information that show unfavorable trends have been identified. Confirm that data from these sources are analyzed to identify potential product and quality problems that may require preventive action.*

Determine whether the firm is identifying product and quality problems that may require a preventive action. This can be accomplished by reviewing historical records such as trending data, corrective actions, acceptance activities (component history records, process control records, finished device testing, and so on), and other quality system records for unfavorable trends. Review if preventive actions have been taken regarding unfavorable trends recognized from the analysis of product and quality information. Product and quality improvements and use of appropriate statistical process control techniques are evidence of compliance with the preventive action requirement.

Determine whether the firm is capturing and analyzing data regarding in-conformance product. Examples include capturing and analyzing component test results to detect shifts in test results that may indicate changes in vendor processes, component design, or acceptance procedures. Identification of these indicators may necessitate a vendor investigation as a preventive action. Monitoring in-process and finished device test results may reveal additional indicators of potential quality problems. For devices where stability is an issue, test results of reserve samples are continually monitored. These monitoring activities may trigger process changes, additional training activities, and other changes required to maintain the process within its tolerances and limits.

Determine whether the firm is using statistical control techniques for process controls where statistical techniques are applicable. An example would be statistical process control (SPC). SPC is utilized to monitor a process and initiate process correction when a process is drifting toward a specification limit. Typically, SPC activities are encountered with large-volume production processes such as plastic molding and extrusion. Any continuing product improvements (in the absence of identified product problems such as nonconforming product) are also positive indicators of preventive actions.

4. *Challenge the quality data information system. Verify that the data received by the CAPA system are complete, accurate, and timely.*

Select one or two quality data sources. Determine whether the data are complete, accurate, and entered into the CAPA system in a timely manner.

5. *Verify that appropriate statistical methods are employed (where necessary) to detect recurring quality problems. Determine whether results of analyses are compared across different data sources to identify and develop the extent of product and quality problems.*

The analysis of product and quality problems should include appropriate statistical and non-statistical techniques. Statistical techniques include Pareto analysis, spreadsheets, and pie charts. Non-statistical techniques include quality review boards, quality review committees, and other methods.

The analysis of product and quality problems should also include the comparison of problems and trends across different data sources to establish a global view of a problem and not an isolated view. For example, problems noted in service records should be compared with similar problem trends noted in complaints and acceptance activity information. The full extent of a problem must be captured before the probability of occurrence, risk analysis, and the proper course of corrective or preventive action can be determined.

6. *Determine whether failure investigation procedures are followed. Determine whether the degree to which a quality problem or nonconforming product is investigated is commensurate with the significance and risk of the nonconformity. Determine whether failure investigations are conducted to determine root cause (where possible). Verify that there is control for preventing distribution of nonconforming product.*

Review the firm's CAPA procedures for conducting failure investigations. Determine whether the procedures include provisions for identifying the failure modes and determining the significance of the failure modes (using tools such as risk analysis). What is the rationale for determining whether a failure analysis should be conducted as part of the investigation, and the depth of the failure analysis?

Discuss with the firm their rationale for determining whether a corrective or preventive action is necessary for an identified trend regarding product or quality problems. The decision process may be linked to the results of a risk analysis and essential device outputs.

Using the sampling tables, select failure investigation records regarding more than one failure mode (if possible) and determine whether the firm is following its failure investigation procedures.

Confirm that all of the failure modes from your selected sample of failure investigations have been captured within data summaries such as reports, pie charts, spreadsheets, Pareto charts, and so on.

Where possible, determine whether the depth of the investigation is sufficient (root cause) to determine the action necessary to correct the problem. Select one significant failure investigation that resulted in a corrective action and determine whether the root cause had been identified so that verification or validation of the corrective action could be accomplished.

Using the sampling tables, review a number of incomplete failure investigations for potential unresolved product nonconformances and potential distribution of nonconforming product. Unresolved problems that could be of significant risk to the patient or user may require product recall if the problem cannot be resolved.

Using the sampling tables, review records regarding nonconforming product where the firm concluded corrective or preventive action was not necessary. As noted above, verify that the firm is not continuing to distribute nonconforming product. This may be an important deficiency based on the class of, and the risk associated with, the product.

Using the sampling tables, review nonconforming product and quality concessions. Review controls for preventing distribution of nonconforming products. Product and quality concessions should be reviewed to verify that the concessions have been made appropriate to product risk and within the requirements of the quality system, not solely to fulfill marketing needs.

7. *Determine whether appropriate actions have been taken for significant product and quality problems identified from data sources.*

Where appropriate, this may include recall actions, changes in acceptance activities for components, in-process and finished devices, and so on.

Using the sampling tables, select and review significant corrective actions and determine whether the change or changes could have extended beyond the action taken. A significant action would be a product or process change to correct a reliability problem or to bring the product into conformance with product specifications. Discuss with the firm their rationale for not extending the action to include additional actions such as changes in component supplier, training, changes to acceptance activities, field action, or other applicable actions. Investigators should discuss and evaluate these issues but be careful not to say anything that could be construed as requesting a product recall.

8. *Determine whether corrective and preventive actions were effective and verified or validated prior to implementation. Confirm that corrective and preventive actions do not adversely affect the finished device.*

Using the selected sample of significant corrective and preventive actions, determine the effectiveness of these corrective or preventive actions. This can be accomplished by reviewing product and quality problem trend results. Determine whether there are any similar products or quality problems after the implementation of the corrective or preventive actions. Determine whether the firm has verified or validated the corrective or preventive actions to ensure that such actions are effective and do not adversely affect the finished device.

Corrective actions must be verified and (if applicable) validated. Corrective actions must include the application of design controls if appropriate.

Good engineering principles should include: establishment of a verification or validation protocol; verification of product output against documented product requirements and specifications; assurance that test instruments are maintained and calibrated; and assurance that test results are maintained, available, and readable.

9. *Verify that corrective and preventive actions for product and quality problems were implemented and documented.*

Using the sampling tables, select and review records of the most recent corrective or preventive actions (this sample may consist of or include records from the previously-selected sample of significant corrective actions). To determine whether corrective and preventive actions for product and quality problems and changes have been documented and implemented, it may be necessary to view actual processes, equipment, facilities, or documentation.

10. *Determine whether information regarding nonconforming product and quality problems and corrective and preventive actions has been properly disseminated, including dissemination for management review.*

Determine that the relevant information regarding quality problems, as well as corrective and preventive actions, has been submitted for management review. This can be accomplished by determining which records in a recent CAPA event were submitted for management review. Review the raw data submitted for management review and not the actual results of a management review.

Review the CAPA (and other procedures if necessary) and confirm that there is a mechanism to disseminate relevant CAPA information to those individuals directly responsible for assuring product quality and the prevention of quality problems.

Review information related to product and quality problems that have been disseminated to those individuals directly responsible for assuring product quality and the prevention of quality problems. Using the sample of records from objective 9 above, confirm that information related to product and quality problems is disseminated to individuals directly responsible for assuring product quality and the prevention of quality problems.

2.4 FDA GUIDANCE: INVESTIGATING OUT-OF-SPECIFICATION (OOS) TEST RESULTS FOR PHARMACEUTICAL PRODUCTION

Originally published in 1998 as draft guidance, this document was finally published in 2006. It derived somewhat from the previously mentioned *Barr* case. The guidance document covers such topics as:

- How to investigate OOS test results
- The laboratory phase of the investigations
- Responsibilities of analyst and supervisor and other laboratory personnel
- When to expand the investigation outside the laboratory to include the production process and raw materials
- Additional testing that may be necessary
- The final evaluation of all test results

Although this guidance applies to chemistry-based laboratory testing of drugs regulated by the Center for Drug Evaluation and Research (CDER), it is one of the few FDA documents that make clear to regulated industries the expectation and interpretation of the FDA (the "how to do" things) regarding failure investigation. What may be one of its most important parts is found within the footnote on page six, which states:

> Please note that §211.192 requires a thorough investigation of any discrepancy, including documentation of conclusions and

> follow-up. Implicit in this requirement for investigation is the need to implement corrective and preventive actions. Corrective and preventive action is consistent with the FDA's requirements under 21 CFR part §820, Subpart J, pertaining to medical devices, as well as the 2004[2] draft guidance entitled *Quality Systems Approach to Pharmaceutical Current Good Manufacturing Practice Regulations,* which, when finalized, will represent the Agency's current thinking on this topic.

In other words, the FDA's expectation is that an investigation and CAPA system similar to the one included in the medical device regulation be implemented by all regulated industry.

OOS Guidance Phase I: Laboratory Investigations

Whenever laboratory error is identified, the firm should determine the source of that error and take corrective action to prevent recurrence. To ensure full compliance with the CGMP regulations, the manufacturer also should maintain adequate documentation of the corrective action.

Unfortunately, most laboratory failures are assigned to analyst errors (for example, due to a procedure not followed) and corrected by some kind of training intervention. For an in-depth analysis of this topic, refer to Chapter 5 and Chapter 6.11. A recent laboratory investigation I reviewed invalidated the failing results, merely establishing that "the original OOS could have been related with an error during the original sampling preparation."

The guidance also states that "laboratory error should be relatively rare. Frequent errors suggest a problem that might be due to inadequate training of analysts, poorly maintained or improperly calibrated equipment, or careless work. Whenever laboratory error is identified, the firm should determine the source of that error and take corrective action to prevent recurrence. To ensure full compliance with the CGMP regulations, the manufacturer also should maintain adequate documentation of the corrective action."

OOS Guidance Phase II: Full Scale OOS Investigation

When the initial assessment does not determine that a laboratory error caused the OOS result and testing results appear to be accurate, a full-scale OOS investigation using a predefined procedure should be conducted. This investigation may consist of a production process review and/or additional laboratory work. The objective of such an investigation should be to identify the root causes of the OOS result and take appropriate corrective and preventive actions. A full-scale investigation should include a review of production and sampling

[2] This guidance was finally published September 2006.

procedures and will often include additional laboratory testing. Such investigations should be given the highest priority. Among the elements of this phase is an evaluation of the impact of OOS results on already distributed batches.

A full-scale OOS investigation should consist of a timely, thorough, and well-documented review that includes the following information:

1. A clear statement of the reason for the investigation
2. A summary of the aspects of the manufacturing process that may have caused the problem
3. The results of a documentation review, with the assignment of actual or probable causes
4. The results of a review made to determine whether the problem has occurred previously
5. A description of corrective actions taken

If this part of the OOS investigation confirms the OOS result and is successful in identifying its root causes, the OOS investigation may be terminated and the product rejected. However, a failure investigation that extends to other batches or products that may have been associated with the specific failure must be completed (§211.192).

A full-scale OOS investigation may include additional laboratory testing. It can be accomplished by retesting a portion of the original sample and/or resampling. It is not infrequent that some companies use a strategy of repeated testing until a passing result is obtained, then disregarding the OOS results without scientific justification. This practice is known as "testing into compliance" and it is unscientific and objectionable under CGMP as well as being one prime reason of regulatory nightmares. The guidance establishes that the maximum number of retests to be performed on a sample should be specified in advance in a written standard operating procedure. The number may vary depending upon the variability of the particular test method employed, but should always be based on scientifically sound principles.

2.5 FDA GUIDANCE: QUALITY SYSTEMS APPROACH TO PHARMACEUTICAL CURRENT GOOD MANUFACTURING PRACTICE REGULATIONS

This guidance describes the aim of the FDA to bring the pharmaceutical GMPs to the level of the medical devices QSR. The introduction section of the guidance clearly establishes this purpose:

> This guidance is intended to help manufacturers implementing modern quality systems and risk management approaches to meet the requirements of the Agency's current good manufacturing practice (cGMP) regulations (21 CFR Parts §210 and 211). The guidance describes a comprehensive quality systems (QS) model, highlighting the model's consistency with the regulatory requirements for manufacturing human and veterinary drugs, including biological drug products. The guidance also explains how manufacturers implementing such quality systems can be in full compliance with parts §210 and 211.

The guidance describes that CAPA is a well-known CGMP regulatory concept that focuses on investigating, understanding, and correcting discrepancies while attempting to prevent their recurrence. Quality system models discuss CAPA as three separate concepts, all of which are used in this guidance:

- Remedial corrections of an identified problem
- Root cause analysis with corrective action to help understand the cause of the deviation and potentially prevent recurrence of a similar problem
- Preventive action to avert recurrence of a similar potential problem

Under corrective action, the guidance establishes:

> This document states that corrective action is a reactive tool for system improvement to ensure that significant problems do not recur. Both quality systems and the CGMP regulations emphasize corrective actions. Quality systems approaches call for procedures to be developed and documented to ensure that the need for action is evaluated relevant to the possible consequences, the root causes of the problem are investigated, possible actions are determined, selected actions are taken within defined time frames, and the effectiveness of the actions taken is evaluated. It is essential to document corrective actions taken (CGMP also requires this; see §211.192).

Examples of sources that can be used to gather such information include the following:

- Nonconformance reports and rejections
- Returns
- Complaints
- Internal and external audits

- Data and risk assessment related to operations and quality system processes
- Management review decisions

For preventive actions:

> Being proactive is an essential tool in quality systems management. Succession planning, training, capturing institutional knowledge, and planning for personnel, policy, and process changes are preventive actions that will help ensure that potential problems and root causes are identified, possible consequences assessed, and appropriate actions considered.

The selected preventive action should be evaluated and recorded, and the system should be monitored for the effectiveness of the action. Problems can be anticipated and their occurrence prevented by reviewing data and analyzing risks associated with operational and quality system processes, and by keeping abreast of changes in scientific developments and regulatory requirements.

2.6 EUROPEAN PHARMACEUTICAL GMP (*EUDRALEX* VOLUME 4)

EudraLex is the collection of rules and regulations governing medicinal products in the European Union. Volume 4 contains guidance for the interpretation of the principles and guidelines of good manufacturing practices for medicinal products for human and veterinary use. There are several instances within directive 2003/94/EC referring to investigation and CAPA system:

Article 10: Production

1. The different production operations shall be carried out in accordance with pre-established instructions and procedures and in accordance with good manufacturing practices. Adequate and sufficient resources shall be made available for the in process controls. All process deviations and product defects shall be documented and thoroughly investigated.

Article 14: Self-inspection

> The manufacturer shall conduct repeated self-inspections as part of the quality assurance system in order to monitor the implementation and respect of good manufacturing practice and to propose any necessary corrective measures. Records shall be maintained of such self-inspections and any corrective action subsequently taken.

EudraLex Volume 4, Chapter 1, Pharmaceutical Quality System revised 2013, refers to investigations and CAPA in four areas:

Pharmaceutical Quality System

1.4 (ix) The results of product and processes monitoring are taken into account in batch release, in the investigation of deviations, and, with a view to taking preventive action to avoid potential deviations occurring in the future.

Good Manufacturing Practice for Medicinal Products

1.8 (vi) Records are made, manually and/or by recording instruments, during manufacture which demonstrate that all the steps required by the defined procedures and instructions were in fact taken and that the quantity and quality of the product was as expected.

1.8 (vii) Any significant deviations are fully recorded and investigated with the objective of determining the root cause and appropriate corrective and preventive action implemented.

1.8 (xi) Complaints about products are examined, the causes of quality defects investigated and appropriate measures taken in respect of the defective products and to prevent reoccurrence.

Quality Control

1.9 (vi) Records are made of the results of inspections and that testing of materials, intermediate, bulk, and finished products is formally assessed against specification. Product assessment includes a review and evaluation of relevant production documentation and an assessment of deviations from specified procedures.

Product Quality Review

1.10 (iv) A review of all significant deviations or nonconformances, their related investigations, and the effectiveness of resultant corrective and preventive actions taken.

1.10 (viii) A review of all quality-related returns, complaints and recalls and the investigations performed at the time.

1.10 (ix) A review of adequacy of any other previous product process or equipment corrective actions.

1.11 The manufacturer and, where different, marketing authorization holder, should evaluate the results of this review and an assessment made of whether corrective and preventive action or any revalidation should be undertaken, under the Pharmaceutical Quality System.

> There should be management procedures for the ongoing management and review of these actions and the effectiveness of these procedures verified during self-inspection. Quality reviews may be grouped by product type, for example. solid dosage forms, liquid dosage forms, sterile products, etc. where scientifically justified.

2.7 HARMONIZATION PROCESSES: ICH AND GHTF/IMDRF

The International Conference on Harmonization of Technical Requirements for Registration of Pharmaceuticals for Human Use (ICH) brings together the regulatory authorities of Europe, Japan, and the United States and experts from the pharmaceutical industry in the three regions to discuss scientific and technical aspects of product registration. The purpose is to make recommendations on ways to achieve greater harmonization in the interpretation and application of technical guidelines and requirements for product registration in order to reduce or obviate the need to duplicate the testing carried out during the research and development of new medicines. The objective of such harmonization is a more economical use of human, animal, and material resources and the elimination of unnecessary delay in the global development and availability of new medicines at the same time as maintaining safeguards on quality, safety and efficacy, and regulatory obligations to protect public health.

The Global Harmonization Task Force (GHTF) was a voluntary group of representatives from national medical device regulatory authorities (such as the U.S. FDA) and the members of the medical device industry whose goal is the standardization of medical device regulation across the world. The representatives from its five founding members (the European Union, the United States, Canada, Japan, and Australia) were divided into three geographical areas: Europe, Asia-Pacific, and North America. Each of these actively regulates medical devices using its own unique regulatory framework. Founded in 1992, the GHTF was created by EU, US, Japanese, Australian and Canadian regulatory and industry officials in an effort to respond to the growing need for international harmonization in the regulation of medical devices. In November 2012, the global medical device harmonization body ceased its activities, leaving its unfinished work to the International Medical Device Regulators Forum (IMDRF), a successor organization comprised of officials from regulatory agencies—not industry—around the world. The organization had been a mainstay among the regulatory harmonization movement.

2.8 ICH Q10: PHARMACEUTICAL QUALITY SYSTEM

The ICH Q10 document on pharmaceutical quality systems was adopted at step 4 of the process at the ICH steering committee meeting in June 2008. At step 4 the final draft was recommended for adoption to the regulatory bodies of the European Union, Japan, and United States. It describes the CAPA system as follows:

> The pharmaceutical company should have a system for implementing corrective actions and preventive actions resulting from the investigation of complaints, product rejections, non-conformances, recalls, deviations, audits, regulatory inspections and findings, and trends from process performance and product quality monitoring. A structured approach to the investigation process should be used with the objective of determining root cause. The level of effort and formality of the investigation should be commensurate with the level of risk. CAPA methodology should result in product and process improvements and enhanced product and process understanding.

2.9 ISO 13485 AND NON-U.S. MEDICAL DEVICE REGULATIONS

Main non-U.S. regulations (European Community, Canada, and Japan) for medical devices are basically aligned (harmonized) with the ISO 13485 standard. ISO 13485:2003 *Medical devices—Quality management systems—Requirements for regulatory purposes* has become the world standard for medical device quality systems and it was complemented by the publishing of ISO/TR 14969:2004 *Medical devices—Quality management systems—Guidance on the application of ISO 13485:2003.*

Canada has adopted ISO 13485:2003 as a Canadian national standard and labeled it CAN/CSA-ISO 13485:2003. In Europe it was adopted as EN ISO 13485:2003 and updated on January 21, 2012 as EN ISO 13485:2012. The text of the global standard ISO 13485:2003 is unchanged, only the foreword and annexes in the European version have been revised.[3] It is not mandatory to use EN ISO 13485 as the quality system standard, but any required system must be equivalent to this or better; even the low risk Class I devices benefit from a quality system that is in effect the core management system for a medical device company.

---

[3] An updated version of the ISO 13485 standard is expected during 2016.

Investigation and CAPA requirements within ISO 13485:2003

Sections 8.5 Improvement and 8.5.1 General require the organization to continuously improve the QMS. Such improvement can be implemented and maintained through the use of corrective and preventive processes, among others.

Under 8.5.2 *Corrective action*, the standard establishes that:

> The organization shall take action to eliminate the cause of nonconformities in order to prevent recurrence. Corrective actions shall be appropriate to the effects of the nonconformities encountered. A documented procedure shall be established to define requirements for
>
> a. Reviewing nonconformities (including customer complaints),
>
> b. Determining the causes of nonconformities,
>
> c. Evaluating the need for action to ensure that nonconformities do not recur,
>
> d. Determining and implementing action needed, including, if appropriate, updating documentation,
>
> e. Recording of the results of any investigation and of action taken, and
>
> f. Reviewing corrective action taken and its effectiveness.

Similarly, for 8.5.3 *Preventive action*:

> The organization shall determine action to eliminate the causes of potential nonconformities in order to prevent their occurrence. Preventive actions shall be appropriate to the effects of the potential problems. A documented procedure shall be established to define requirements for
>
> a. Determining potential nonconformities and their causes,
>
> b. Evaluating the need for action to prevent occurrence of nonconformities,
>
> c. Determining and implementing action needed, and
>
> d. Recording of the results of any investigations and of action taken, and reviewing preventive action taken and its effectiveness.

When comparing ISO 13485:2003 requirements with the content of the FDA QSR 21 CFR §820.100, the conclusion is that the intent of each document is consistent with the other in terms of the corrective and preventive action system. It can be concluded that the requirements established by the QSR are far more prescriptive.

Regarding control of nonconforming product, FDA's QSR provides more detail as to the items to be recorded in a nonconforming product situation. It explicitly addresses the need for an investigation in such a situation.

Investigation and CAPA requirements within the new version of ISO 13485

A new version of the ISO 13485 is at its final review and approval stage and it should be released during 2016. Basically, the intent of this new version is to better align this standard with the ISO 9001. However, the new ISO 13485 is being aligned to ISO 9001:2008, not to the new ISO 9001:2015 version. Several changes will be introduced to control of nonconforming product and corrective action and preventive action clauses. Among them:

- 8.2 under Monitoring and Measuring establishes that trending data will be required to be reviewed, analyzed and determine if applicable to enter CAPA process.
- 8.2.1.2.1—New Section on Complaint Handling—requires procedures for complaint handling, investigation, and regulatory notification.
- 8.2.1.2.2—New Section on reporting—requires procedures and records for reporting to regulatory authorities.
- 8.3 under control of nonconforming product now requires that nonconforming product shall be considered for corrective action. Four new sections are included under this clause to cover general control of nonconforming products, and control of nonconforming products before delivery to customer, after delivery, and rework. The new standard now expects you to investigate nonconforming products that have been delivered, to determine if corrective action is needed, and to consider whether or not responsible external parties need to be notified.
- Under clause 8.5.2 (corrective action) new requirement are included regarding the impact of corrective action with regard to safety and performance.
- For preventive action (clause 8.5.3) new requirement are included regarding timeliness of preventive action and consideration of the impact to QMS and regulatory requirement for preventive action.

2.10 GHTF QUALITY MANAGEMENT SYSTEM—MEDICAL DEVICES—GUIDANCE ON CORRECTIVE ACTION AND PREVENTIVE ACTION AND RELATED QMS PROCESSES

The scope of this document is to "provide guidance for establishing adequate processes for measurement, analysis, and improvement within the QMS as related to correction and/or corrective action for nonconformities or preventive action for potential nonconformities of systems, processes or products."

It also states that "the document is intended for medical device manufacturers and regulatory authorities. It is intended for educational purposes and is not intended to be used to assess or audit compliance with regulatory requirements. For this purpose the manufacturer will establish processes and define appropriate controls for measurement and analysis to identify nonconformities and potential nonconformities. The manufacturer should have established processes defining when and how corrections, corrective actions, or preventive actions should be undertaken. These actions should be commensurate with the significance or risk of the nonconformity or potential nonconformity."

Curiously, the task force decided that the acronym "CAPA" will not be used in the document because "the concept of corrective action and preventive action has been incorrectly interpreted to assume that a preventive action is required for every corrective action. This document will discuss the escalation process from different 'reactive' sources which will be corrective in nature and other 'proactive' sources which will be preventive in nature. The manufacturer is required to account for both types of data sources whether they are of a corrective or preventive nature."

2.11 COMPLAINT INVESTIGATIONS: REGULATORY EXPECTATIONS AND BEST PRACTICES

Complaint investigation is very often the beginning point of every regulatory inspection to determine whether the company has received complaints of possible (or potentially) defective products because complaints may provide leads in identifying product and/or quality defects. Pharmaceutical CGMP and medical devices QS regulation requires all complaints be reviewed, evaluated and maintained by a formally designated unit. This unit must decide whether an investigation of the complaint needs to be performed.

Deficiencies in complaint handling practices may result in lost complaint data essential to identifying product defects, and possibly quality system problems, which have not been adequately corrected by the firm. Possible corrective actions may include recall, and/or change in the design of the device, and/or change in the manufacturing process or quality system. Inspectors will also determine if the firm has performed sufficient complaint investigation, or to the extent possible, to confirm the reported failure mode.

Each regulated company needs to evaluate complaints thoroughly to determine whether an investigation is necessary. Indicators that the company may not be in compliance would be shown by:

- A history of one or more similar failure modes that has not been investigated to confirm the reported failure mode.
- The complaint records lack the reason for not investigating and/or the name of the individual responsible for the decision not to investigate.

§211.198 describes complaint files for drugs and establishes that:

(a) Written procedures describing the handling of all written and oral complaints regarding a drug product shall be established and followed. Such procedures shall include provisions for review by the quality control unit, of any complaint involving the possible failure of a drug product to meet any of its specifications and, for such drug products, a determination as to the need for an investigation in accordance with 211.192. Such procedures shall include provisions for review to determine whether the complaint represents a serious and unexpected adverse drug experience which is required to be reported to the FDA in accordance with 310.305 and 514.80 of this chapter.

(b)(2) Where an investigation under 211.192 is conducted, the written record shall include the findings of the investigation and follow-up. The record or copy of the record of the investigation shall be maintained at the establishment where the investigation occurred in accordance with 211.180(c).

(b)(3) Where an investigation under 211.192 is not conducted, the written record shall include the reason that an investigation was found not to be necessary and the name of the responsible person making such a determination.

§820.198 describes complaint files for medical devices and establishes that:

(b) Each manufacturer shall review and evaluate all complaints to determine whether an investigation is necessary. When no investigation is made, the manufacturer shall maintain a record that includes the reason no investigation was made and the name of the individual responsible for the decision not to investigate.

(c) Any complaint involving the possible failure of a device, labeling, or packaging to meet any of its specifications shall be reviewed, evaluated, and investigated, unless such investigation has already been performed for a similar complaint and another investigation is not necessary.

(e) When an investigation is made under this section, a record of the investigation shall be maintained by the formally designated unit identified in paragraph (a) of this section.

2.12 CURRENT OBSERVATIONS AND REGULATORY TRENDS FOR INVESTIGATIONS AND CAPA SYSTEM

Investigation and CAPA remain two of the most frequent categories of regulatory citation in the US and elsewhere.

U.S. FDA Drug (21 CFR 211)

During fiscal year 2015 (October 2014 to September 2015), FDA issued a total of 678 Form 483s (forms indicating areas of noncompliance at a facility) to pharmaceutical companies. A total of 3506 observation were related to finished pharmaceuticals CGMP with 344 of them related to the investigation and CAPA system, specifically related to complaint and production investigations. It is important to remember that the U.S. FDA CGMP for finished pharmaceutical does not explicitly include a CAPA subpart of section, and for this reason, observations related to CAPA are scattered thorough the whole CGMP sections as described in section 2.1.

U.S. FDA Medical Devices (21 CFR 820)

During fiscal year 2015 (October 2014 to September 2015), FDA issued a total of 1008 Form 483s (forms indicating areas of noncompliance at a facility) to medical device companies. A total of 3599 observation were related to quality system regulations with 1133 of them related to the investigation and CAPA system, including complaint investigations.

Following are some examples of U.S. FDA observations related to investigations and CAPA:

- Your firm performs corrective actions in the Product Risk Assessment (PRA) system, the Nonconformance (NCR) system and the Equipment/Instrument Calibration (OOT) system; the corrective actions taken in these systems do not include conducting verifications of effectiveness to the specific correction to ensure the problem was resolved, reoccurrence was prevented, and the action did not negatively affect the finished device.

- Your firm has no CAPA procedures as defined in the QS regulation including: failure investigation, procedures to analyze quality data...procedures to verify/validate corrections, procedures that ensure that information related to quality problems is disseminated and for submitting relevant information on identified quality problems to management for review.
- Based upon the investigation of the cause of irradiation batches receiving doses below the specified minimum dose requirement (due to incorrect packaging and product density), the firm implemented new packaging procedures and retrained employees. Irradiation batches receiving doses below the specified minimum dose requirement have recurred after implementation of the cited corrective action. The firm's management stated that the recurring nonconformities may be attributed to employees not following directions.
- Your Quality Assurance review of critical and major complaint investigations (Technical Complaint Investigation Reports) is not occurring in a timely manner according to your procedures. As of 12/12/11, your firm is overdue (untimely) with adequately conducting approximately 1,360 investigations you have received from consumer complaints (1,332 are major, 31 are critical). This backlog of overdue complaints has been over 1,000 in number since at least 8/30/11. Complaints· requiring review include, but are not limited to: foreign products in container, suspected tampering, foreign object, missing label, discolored product, partial tablet, chipped/cracked and crumbled product.

Data published from MHRA (UK's medicines and healthcare products regulatory agency) for year 2013[4] establishes that investigation of anomalies remains the most cited inspection deficiency during the last five years (from 2009 to 2013). CAPA was the third most cited deficiency during year 2013. Following are some examples of these two categories:

Investigation of anomalies

- The management of "high" risk deviations was deficient. The investigation into 2 positive sterility tests recovered in November 2011 was not complete at the time of the inspection; only a one-page interim report was available on day one of the inspection.
- There were multiple examples from the inspection where deviations had not been raised in circumstances where the procedures in place indicated that such documentation was required.

[4] https://www.gov.uk/government/uploads/system/uploads/attachment_data/file/448609/Good_manufacturing_practice_inspection_deficiencies_2013.pdf

- On-going serious deviations (related to human operational failures) had not been resolved in a robust and timely manner.
- There was no justification from the findings for the retraining of manufacturing staff. A number of the investigations appeared to place an over reliance on retraining in the absence of a critical review of systems and supporting documentation in place at the time of the incident.
- The procedure allowed up to 60 days for the completion of the investigations categorized as critical. This was considered too long to ensure a timely review and impact assessment to be performed.
- The procedure did not detail a system for reviewing of overdue investigation and an appropriate extension process.
- A large number of investigations were seen that were not closed in a timely manner or were still open a number of months beyond the stipulated expected closure time. There was no assessment of the impact of these overdue investigations and no assessment as to the root cause of the failure to follow the procedure.
- A number of investigations were seen that did not include detailed robust root cause investigation. Therefore, potential impacts were not fully assessed and the root cause and subsequent CAPA were not robust.

CAPA

- There was a lack of a robust investigation for the reviewed compounding complaints and nonconformances designed to identify root cause and hence appropriate actions to minimize the potential for reoccurrence. It was noted that the frequent use of terms such as "human error," "isolated occurrence," and "no trend" appeared to limit the investigation conducted.
- Root cause, implications for other batches, CAPA and batch disposition were not clearly defined.
- The site had failed to investigate effective remedial actions in a number of areas as evidenced by deficiencies raised at this inspection being of a similar nature to those raised at previous MHRA inspections. This indicated that the quality management system was focused on dealing with the specifics of the deficiency rather than taking a holistic view to enable the quality management system and site practices to be strengthened.

3

ISO 9001:2015—Nonconformance and CAPA requirements

ISO 9001, the fundamental international QMS standard, has been recently revised under the new version ISO 9001:2015.[1] Changes included in the new version are so much more significant than those in the 2008 version. This standard now follows the harmonized structure (known as Annex SL) that will be followed by many other ISO standards. It requires that top management promote the use of risk-based thinking in addition to a process approach. One of the key purposes of implementing a QMS is to act as a preventive tool. As a result, the formal requirement related to preventive action (existing since the version of ISO 9001:1994) was removed from this version and replaced with the risk-based thinking.

Preventive action is no longer part of the new ISO 9001:2015 because it was associated with corrective action since the ISO 9001:1994 version (see Table 1.3), which is not truly an effective planning function. ISO 9001:2015 emphasizes proactive error-proofing processes to prevent problems from occurring because detection (along with root cause identification and corrective action implementation) is not as effective as it should be. Therefore, the aim of the new standard is that planning the QMS upfront is the best preventive action, making a clause tied to corrective action unnecessary.

The former corrective action clause (8.5.2 in ISO 9001:2008) has been replaced by a new clause named "Nonconformity and corrective action" (10.2), while the preventive action clause (8.5.3 in ISO 9001:2008) has been deleted and its spirit has been incorporated as part of a new clause (6.1) named "Action to address risks and opportunities."

The 2015 version requires an organization to react to nonconformity and, as applicable, make corrections, evaluate the need for corrective action to eliminate the cause of the nonconformity, implement any action needed, review the effectiveness of the corrective action, and make changes to the QMS. Clause 8.5.1 includes as a requirement the "implementation of actions to prevent human error."

---

[1] *ISO 9001:2015 Quality management systems—Requirements*

Clause 8.7, named "Control of nonconforming outputs," includes under clause 8.7.1.:

> The organization shall ensure that outputs that do not conform to their requirements are identified and controlled to prevent their unintended use or delivery. The organization shall take appropriate action based on the nature of the nonconformity and its effect on the conformity of products and services. This shall also apply to nonconforming products and services detected after delivery of products, during or after the provision of services.
>
> The organization shall deal with nonconforming outputs in one or more of the following ways:
>
> a) correction;
>
> b) segregation, containment, return or suspension of provision of products and services;
>
> c) informing the customer;
>
> d) obtaining authorization for acceptance under concession.

Conformity to the requirements shall be verified when nonconforming outputs are corrected.

Under clause 8.7.2 the new standard establishes that "the organization shall retain documented information that:

> a) describes the nonconformity;
>
> b) describes the actions taken;
>
> c) describes any concessions obtained;
>
> d) identifies the authority deciding the action in respect of the nonconformity.

The spirit of the new ISO 9001:2015 is already present in concepts such as pharmaceutical's quality by design and medical device's design controls. Risk-based thinking and preventive actions are key parts of the design and development process. Moreover, the strong emphasis on risk management in this new version of the standard has been already embraced by the regulated industry with the incorporation of such concepts through guidances (pharmaceutical's ICH Q9) and standards (ISO 14971 for medical devices or ISO 22000 for food).

Organizations rarely apply the preventive action concept at the optimal stage in a QMS because of cost or time limitations. Preventing every potential problem and nonconformance is prohibitively expensive or even impossible.

ISO 9001:2015's requirement of risk-based thinking can help to prevent major failures and issues, but it's unlikely that it will prevent a vast majority of potential problems. I believe that our current understanding of the preventive action concept (when correctly interpreted and applied) will survive for many years. Who can be opposed to extending any identified improvement to other products, process, or system not yet affected by an identified root cause(s)?

4

Effective Investigation and CAPA Processes: From Problem Detection to Effectiveness Check

This chapter describes sequentially the entire investigation and CAPA processes. It begins with problem detection and associated correction or remedial actions to stop the problem; then continues with root cause investigation, generation, and implementation of corrective and preventive actions, and ends with the evaluation of their effectiveness and the management of the investigation and CAPA systems. Topics such as trending, training effectiveness evaluation, and risk management concepts as they related to investigation and CAPA are discussed in this chapter. Special emphasis is devoted to the investigation of the so-called "human error."

The basic investigation and CAPA process flow is shown in Figure 4.1, while Figure 4.2 describes the different stages and elements of the investigation and CAPA system.

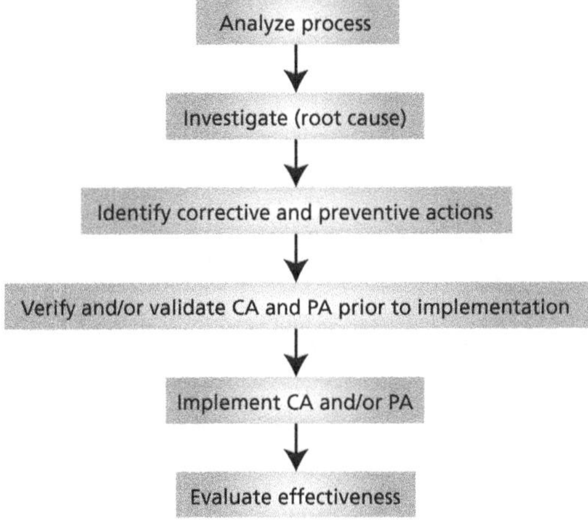

Figure 4.1 The Investigation and CAPA process flow.

As can be seen in Figure 4.2, the entire system is made up of three phases: investigation, CAPA plan, and effectiveness evaluation. One of the major mistakes we have seen is the use of words such as "analyze," "evaluate," "assess," and so on as actions of the CAPA plan phase. None of these actions belong to the CAPA plan phase. In fact, they are part of the extension of the investigation. So, they really belong to the investigation phase, not to the CAPA plan phase.

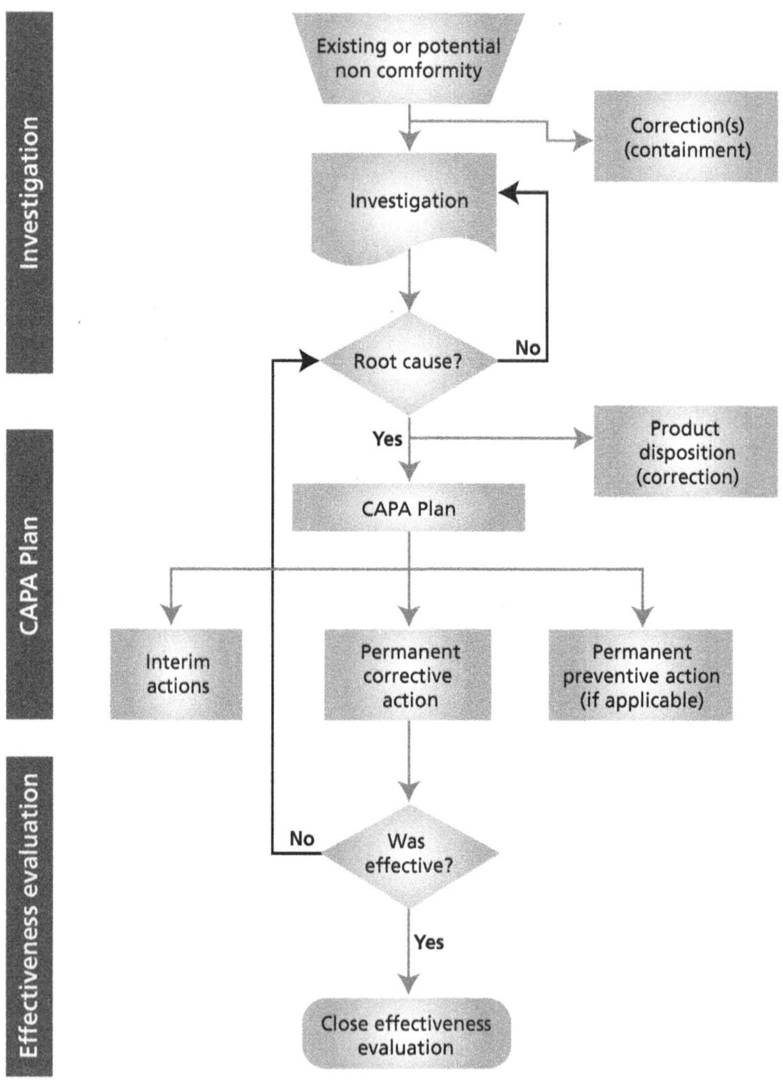

Figure 4.2 The Investigation and CAPA system.

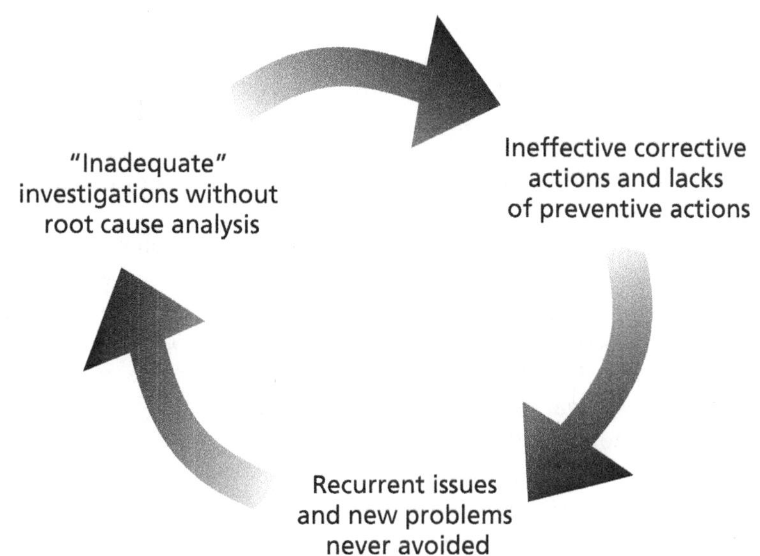

Figure 4.3 The ineffective Investigation and CAPA circle.

As easy as it seems, practically all manufacturers of medical-regulated products are continuously struggling with their investigation and CAPA systems. The main areas of opportunity are depicted in Figure 4.3, which represents the "vicious circle" of investigation and CAPA: lack of adequate root cause analysis leads to ineffective corrective actions, which in turn leads to recurrence of the issues, which leads to the need to investigate again and again the same old issue.

4.1 PROBLEM DETECTION: DISCOVERING PROBLEMS

4.1.1 Source of Data About Product and Quality Issues

As previously mentioned, there is a perception in the life-sciences industry that the investigation and CAPA requirements for U.S. medical devices are far more stringent than any other regulations established either by the FDA or by foreign regulators. Using this regulation as a guideline, there are three areas with requirements related to the identification of quality problems. Section 820.90(a), Control of nonconforming product, establishes that "as part of controlling nonconforming product, each manufacturer needs to evaluate each nonconformance, including a determination of the need for an investigation."

As part of the CAPA subsystem, §820.100(a) states that "each manufacturer needs to analyze processes, work operations, concessions, quality audit reports, quality records, service records, complaints, returned product, and other sources of quality data to identify existing and potential causes of nonconforming product, or other quality problems. Appropriate statistical methodology shall be employed where necessary to detect recurring quality problems."

Finally, §820.198 (complaint files) establishes that "each manufacturer shall review and evaluate all complaints to determine whether an investigation is necessary." This section also clarifies that any complaint involving the possible failure of a device, labeling, or packaging to meet any of its specifications shall be reviewed, evaluated, and investigated, unless such investigation has already been performed for a similar complaint and another investigation is not necessary.

As can be noticed, these three sections are interrelated; that is, they cannot be interpreted alone. Section §820.90(a) establishes that all nonconformities shall be evaluated in order to determine if an investigation is needed. Meanwhile, §820.198 establishes that all complaints shall be evaluated to determine whether an investigation is needed or not. However, §820.198 goes further to require the name of the person responsible and the rationale when an investigation is not performed. Therefore, both sections provide a pathway to opening an investigation (including a root cause analysis, corrective and preventive actions, and effectiveness evaluation) or just simply to implementing corrections and trend monitoring. Figure 4.4 shows the interrelationship of §820.90, §820.100, and §820.198.

CAPA procedures must clearly identify what data sources are being used as input for the CAPA system. A frequent citation during inspections is that "the firm is not using all sources of quality data." Among the main sources we might consider:

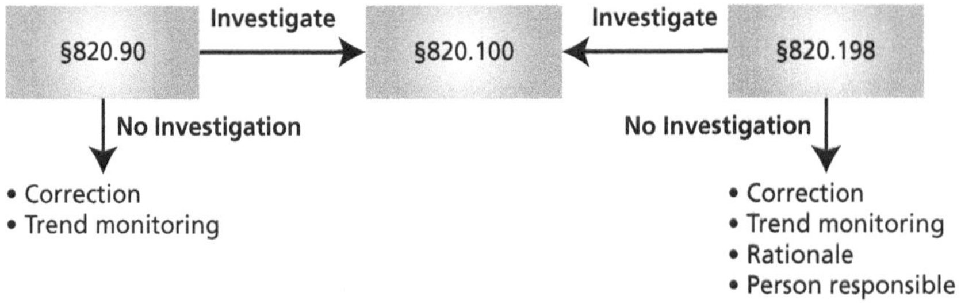

Figure 4.4 Relationship among §820.90, §820.100, and §820.198.

- Acceptance activity records relating to incoming, in-process, and finished product testing
- Stability issues
- External (customer) complaints
- Internal complaints
- FDA 483s, warning letters, and published literature
- Corrective and preventive actions
- Reports of system, process, or product nonconformities
- Process monitoring data (for example, statistical control charts, trends, run charts, yields, and so on)
- Calibration and maintenance records
- Scrap, rework, "Use As Is," and other concessions
- Clinical adverse events
- Quality audit reports (internal, external, supplier, and third-party audits)
- Returned products analysis
- Training

There are additional sources of quality data such as:

- Field alert reports, medical device reports and vigilance reports
- Installation and/or repair (servicing) reports
- Spare parts usage
- Customer and/or technical service requests
- Field service and/or warranty reports
- Customer feedback (for example, surveys)
- Historical records from previous corrections
- Lawsuits and other legal actions

4.1.2 Initial Impact Assessment

A preliminary evaluation of the impact of the event based on the initial data and evidence available is one of the first actions to be taken once a problem is detected. It's important to establish the boundaries of the problem, as soon as possible. If confidence exists that no other material has been affected, it must be supported with objective evidence. We need to consider product (lots/batches) directly affected by the event as well as any other product potentially affected. Special attention must be placed on products that ran before and after the lot under investigation.

One of the most critical questions at this point is to establish whether any material affected by this situation reached the customer.

The preliminary investigation must determine whether any affected materials (in-process product, purchased or manufactured raw materials, or packaging components) have been processed beyond the area in which the situation was identified. If so, these other areas must be included, as appropriate, in the impact assessment.

Until the most probable root causes can be established, *everything is suspicious*. For example, once a product failed a specification:

- Other batches manufactured with the same components could be affected.
- Other batches manufactured / tested with the same equipment could be affected.
- Other batches manufactured / tested by the same operator / analyst could be affected.

Once the root cause is determined (for example, a component caused the failure), we can establish that:

- Other batches manufactured with the same components could be affected.
- Other batches manufactured / tested with the same equipment were not affected.
- Other batches manufactured / tested by the same operator / analyst were not affected.

The requirements for this impact assessment are clearly established in the CGMP (21 CFR §211.192):

> The investigation shall extend to other batches of the same drug product and other drug products that may have been associated with the specific failure or discrepancy. A written record of the investigation shall be made and shall include the conclusions and follow up.

In the landmark judicial decision *United States v Barr Laboratories, Inc. (1993)* there are requirements for listing and evaluating lots potentially affected by the failure under investigation. As a third example, the 2006 FDA guidance on investigation of out of specification establishes that:

> Once the OOS is confirmed, the investigation changes from an OOS investigation into a batch failure investigation, which must be extended to other batches or products that may have been associated with the specific failure (§211.192).

4.1.2.1 Risk Assessment

Risk management concepts have been part of the medical devices world for many years.[1] At first, the regulators used the term "hazard analysis" and it was part of the hazard analysis and critical control point (HACCP) methodology. For the last decade or so, HACCP terminology has been restricted to food safety. Thus, the FDA, ISO, and other regulators embraced the term "risk analysis," which evolved to the current broader term of "risk management." Risk analysis requirements are incorporated only into the design control (§820.30) element of FDA's QSR, but the preamble of this regulation includes mentions about risk analysis expectations across many elements. There is also an ISO standard (ISO 14971:2012), originally issued in 2000 and first revised in 2007. This establishes the risk management requirements to determine the safety of a medical device by the manufacturer during the product life cycle.

For other regulated products, such as drugs, the application of the risk management concepts is very recent. It was done in the form of an international guidance document, ICH Q9 "Quality Risk Management," which was adopted as a non-binding guidance by the drug and biologic centers of the FDA in June 2006.

Having in mind those risk management principles, typical questions must be answered: *Do we always need an investigation? Do we always need corrective and preventive actions? How soon must companies fix their CAPA problems?*

CAPA and risk management are two interlocked concepts that cannot be separated. All of our decisions regarding CAPA must be filtered throughout the risk management system. Let's now answer these questions.

Regarding the first question: *Do we always need an investigation?* The theoretical response is yes. Every time we detect some kind of "problem," it is necessary to look into it. Repeating the primal concept of the investigation and CAPA system, continuous improvement requires the analysis of the issue to discover its root cause before we can implement actions to prevent its recurrence. To be able to fix the cause of the problem, we must first discover its causes. Without some kind of investigation or evaluation, the probability that we can reach the real root causes is low. However, resources are not unlimited (actually they are becoming more and more scarce) and definitively not all issues have the same significance. As the QSR preamble states, "at times a very in depth investigation will be necessary, while at other times a simple investigation, followed by trend analysis or other appropriate tools, will be acceptable." Therefore, we must prioritize and risk assessment is one of the best tools we can use for this purpose. The significance of the product or quality issue can be evaluated by considering the criteria described in Table 4.1.

[1] For an in-depth review of this topic see Rodríguez-Pérez, J. (2012).

Table 4.1 Risk assessment criteria.

Criterion	Categories and Examples
Does it have the potential for a patient or user safety issue?	• **Critical or Catastrophic:** can cause death or significant disability to a patient or user (contaminated injectable drug, critical drug mix-up, contaminated catheter) • **Marginal:** can cause minor injuries to patient or user (overpotent or subpotent drugs, or incorrect diagnoses) • **Negligible:** no injury to patient or user (cosmetic defect, empty box without product)
Type or classification of the product	• Device class I/II • Device class III • Intravenous drug or sterile product • Drug other than intravenous (oral, cutaneous) • Drug with narrow therapeutic ranges • Over-the-counter product
Does it affect the reliability, effectiveness or usability of the product? *Note: consider the worst case*	• Totally affected: not working, not usable or not effective (missing product, broken device) • Partially affected: underfill, low count/quantity • Not affected
Does the issue cause the product to fall outside of established specifications?	• Final specification failure • Non-final specification failure • Incoming acceptance specification • Validity (system suitability) specification
Does it affect the labeling of the product?	• Final label incorrect (lot number, expiration date) • Non-final label incorrect
How frequent is the problem?	• First time occurrence • Occasional • Frequent

(Continued)

(Continued)

Table 4.1 Risk assessment criteria.

Criterion	Categories and Examples
Does the frequency of the occurrence of the issue changed?	• Improving • Worsening
How difficult is to detect the issue?	• Not detectable by manufacturer (customer detected it) • Detected by chance (shipping operator detected it) • Detected by process (inspection detected the failure)
Does it represent a regulatory risk (can this product be considered as adulterated or misbranded?)	• Mix-ups • Product released prior to completion of its record review

Note: Drugs include also biopharmaceutical products

Most regulated companies perform some kind of risk evaluation based on the frequency and the severity (importance, significance) of the event. Situations in which the frequency is rare and the severity is low may not require further investigation. Nevertheless, this evaluation must be documented. In other words, if you can demonstrate (with objective evidence) that the problem has low frequency and no significant danger, then you could pass on this investigation and focus your effort on more significant issues.

The biggest concern with this evaluation is that a vast majority of regulated companies focused the severity evaluation exclusively on the safety of the patient. Based on that evaluation, they assigned very low risk scores to deviations and non-conformances that represent major violations of CGMPs and therefore render such products as adulterated.

Regarding the second question: *Do we always need corrective and preventive actions?* If you investigated and discovered the root causes of the problem, it would be insane not to fix them. The FDA position in this matter can be found on the preamble to the October 7, 1996 Medical Devices QSR. In comment 159 of the preamble, which relates to the degree of corrective or preventive actions, FDA states "FDA cannot dictate in a regulation the degree of action that should be taken because each circumstance will be different, but FDA does expect the manufacturer to develop procedures for assessing the risk, the actions that need to be taken for different levels of risk, and how to correct or prevent the problem from recurring, depending on that risk assessment."

A remarkable observation on this side of the investigation and CAPA system is that many companies always require both corrective and preventive actions even in situations where no preventive action can be applied. In some cases, the reason to require them is simply that the CAPA form includes both type of actions and therefore both are always required.

How soon must companies fix their CAPA problems? The third question refers to the timeliness of failure investigations and corrective or preventive actions. Time frames for completing the different CAPA actions must be established based on the risk of the situation under investigation. In the sixth chapter, we will elaborate on this issue because it constitutes one of the biggest opportunities for improving CAPA systems. One simple approach used by several companies is to complete investigations (this is, the root cause investigation) in four weeks for low-risk situations, three weeks for medium-risk situations, and two weeks for high-risk situations. In the cases previously mentioned, risk classification is normally based on frequency and severity alone.

Our recommendation is to use risk management criteria to determine how deeply and how fast every nonconformance or deviation should be treated. These risk criteria must be clearly defined in written procedures. One example might be establishing who is responsible for evaluating product or quality issues and determining whether a failure investigation is necessary. Another example would be maintaining a record when no failure investigation is made, including the reason and the name of the individual responsible for the decision. The procedure should also determine the depth to which a failure investigation is to be carried out and when an investigation should not pursue corrective action.

Table 4.2 depicts a simple way to carry out this task by segregating nonconformances and deviations into three categories based on the previously described risk criteria. For each situation, an overall risk score is determined by considering the worst-case scenario of the eight dimensions under analysis. Check marks indicate the risk classification that is assigned to each dimension. For example, if the problem can have a critical or catastrophic impact on the safety of the patient, then its risk score must be high independent of any other dimension such as product classification, problem detectability, and so on.

Table 4.2 can be applied to processes and systems, including equipment failure where no product was directly affected.

Table 4.2 Risk assessment score matrix.

Criterion	Categories	RISK SCORE		
		Negligible or Low (1)	Medium (2)	High (3)
Safety	Critical or catastrophic			✔
	Marginal		✔	
	Negligible	✔		
Product classification	Device class I or II	✔		
	Device class III		✔	
	Intravenous drug or sterile product		✔	
	Drug with narrow therapeutic ranges		✔	
	Other drug products or OTC drugs	✔		
Reliability or effectiveness	Totally affected			✔
	Partially affected		✔	
	Not affected	✔		
Product specification	Final specification failure			✔
	Non-final specification failure		✔	
	Specifications are not affected	✔		
Product labeling	Final product labels			✔
	Non-final product labels		✔	
	No labeling is affected	✔		
Frequency or trending	First time occurrence (Isolated event)	✔		
	Occasional but improving	✔		
	Occasional but worsening		✔	
	Frequent		✔	
Detectability	Not detectable or not detected			✔
	Detected by chance		✔	
	Detected by the regular process	✔		
Regulatory risk	Product can be considered as adulterated or misbranded			✔
	Product is not adulterated nor misbranded	✔		

Note: Drugs include also biopharmaceutical products.

Table 4.3 is an example of how to use this risk assessment score matrix for an issue affecting a class III medical device.

Table 4.3 Example of risk assessment.

Criterion	Categories	RISK SCORE		
		Negligible or Low (1)	Medium (2)	High (3)
Safety	Critical or catastrophic			✔
	Marginal		✔	
	Negligible	(✔)		
Product classification	Device class I or II	✔		
	Device class III		(✔)	
	Intravenous drug or sterile product		✔	
	Drug with narrow therapeutic ranges		✔	
	Other drug products or OTC drugs	✔		
Reliability or effectiveness	Totally affected			✔
	Partially affected		✔	
	Not affected	(✔)		
Product specification	Final specification failure			✔
	Non-final specification failure		✔	
	Specifications are not affected	(✔)		
Product labeling	Final product labels			✔
	Non-final product labels		✔	
	No labeling is affected	(✔)		
Frequency or trending	First time occurrence (Isolated event)	(✔)		
	Occasional but improving	✔		
	Occasional but worsening		✔	
	Frequent		✔	
Detectability	Not detectable or not detected			✔
	Detected by chance		✔	
	Detected by the regular process	(✔)		

(Continued)

(Continued)

Table 4.3 Example of risk assessment.

Criterion	Categories	RISK SCORE		
		Negligible or Low (1)	Medium (2)	High (3)
Regulatory risk	Product can be considered as adulterated or misbranded			✔
	Product is not adulterated nor misbranded	✔		

Note: Drugs include also biopharmaceutical products.

A medium risk score was determined for the example above. Now we can use this risk score to determine the content and priority level of each nonconformance investigation as detailed in the Figure 4.5. Table 4.4 describes the characteristics of each nonconformance investigation type.

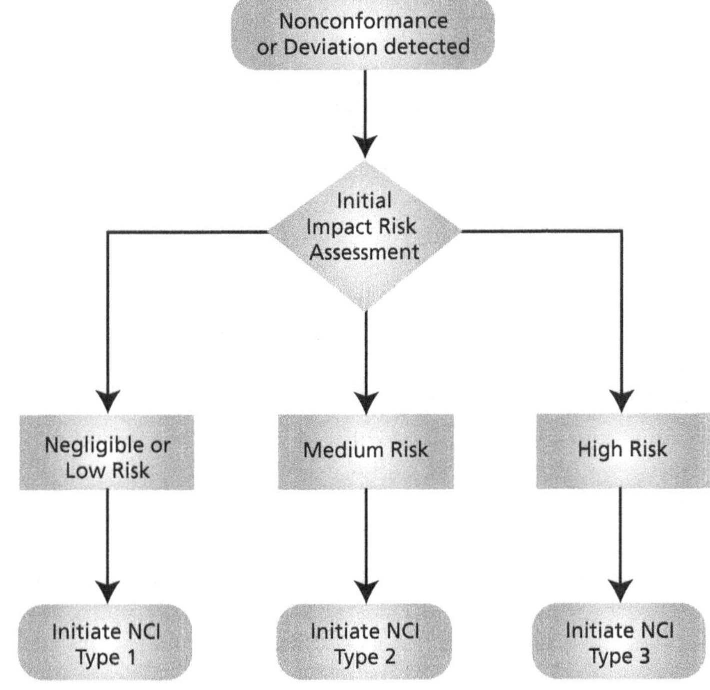

Figure 4.5 Risk prioritization of investigations.

Table 4.4 Type of nonconformance investigations.

Nonconformance Investigation (NCI)		
Type 1	Type 2	Type 3
• Only negligible or low-risk scores are obtained • **Three days** to complete • Document the event and the correction(s) taken • Monthly track and trending of type 1 NCI	• At least one dimension had a medium-risk score • **30 days** to complete • Document the event, root cause analysis, and the correction(s) taken • Need to generate a CAPA Plan	• At least one dimension had a high-risk score • **20 days** to complete • Document the event, root cause analysis, and the correction(s) taken • Need to generate a CAPA Plan

Note: Complete nonconformance investigation means document approval.

4.1.3 Process Trending

Process monitoring is a critical element of continuous improvement. Detection of nonconformances (for example, the failure of a specification) is not an issue in the life-sciences regulated industry, and most of the time failure triggers an investigation within the CAPA system. The problem is the lack of monitoring for in-conformance processes. This is the kind of data that can allow us to identify potential causes of a nonconforming product or other quality problems. Many regulated companies are accustomed to monitoring environmental data, but they do not extend these concepts into the manufacturing or quality control test data. Without process monitoring, the control state expected from a quality management system cannot be achieved.

FDA regulations and guidances contain plenty of requirements and recommendations regarding trending of processes. For medical devices, QSR establishes on §820.100:

a. Each manufacturer shall establish and maintain procedures for implementing corrective and preventive action. The procedures shall include requirements for:

   1. Analyzing processes, work operations, concessions, quality audit reports, quality records, service records, complaints, returned product, and other sources of quality data to identify existing and potential causes of nonconforming product, or other quality problems. Appropriate statistical methodology shall be employed where necessary to detect recurring quality problems.

For pharmaceutical manufacturing, the 2004 FDA Sterile Product Guidance states that "the QCU should provide routine oversight of near-term and long-term trends in environmental and personnel monitoring data." More recently, the landmark 2006 FDA Guidance for Industry Quality Systems Approach to Pharmaceutical Current Good Manufacturing Practice Regulations devoted a whole section to the topic titled *Analyze Data for Trends*:

> Quality systems call for continually monitoring trends and improving systems. This can be achieved by monitoring data and information, identifying and resolving problems, and anticipating and preventing problems. Quality systems procedures involve collecting data from monitoring, measurement, complaint handling, or other activities, and tracking this data over time, as appropriate.
>
> Analysis of data can provide indications that controls are losing effectiveness. The information generated will be essential to achieving problem resolution or problem prevention. Although the CGMP pharmaceutical regulations [§211.180(e)] require product review on at least an annual basis, a quality systems approach calls for trending on a more frequent basis as determined by risk. Trending enables the detection of potential problems as early as possible to plan corrective and preventive actions. Another important concept of modern quality systems is the use of trending to examine processes as a whole; this is consistent with the annual review approach. Trending analyses can help focus internal audits.

Trending relates to process behavior or process stability; process capability relates to the ability of the process to meet the customer specification. Process monitoring reveals the voice of the process. Statistical tools appropriate for this task include run charts, control charts, scatter diagrams, and regression analysis. However, it is important to remark that trending should not be confused with statistical significance. The use of appropriate terminology and wording helps in this task. When we obtain an out-of-specification (OOS), we call it a *failure;* however, when we obtain an out-of-trend (OOT), we call it an *excursion.*

Each company must develop a process monitoring/trending procedure where it must define what an adverse trend is. When an adverse trend is identified, an investigation should be initiated to identify the root cause(s) in order to implement effective corrective and preventive actions.

For environmental monitoring, both short- and long-term trending are used. At least three years of historical data must be kept for the purpose of long-term trending.

Short-term trending:

- Identifies potential drifts from historical results
- Amount required based on risk assessment of potential impact on manufactured products
- Provides daily and weekly excursion trend analysis
- Uses single sample point plots of all critical surfaces, areas, or utilities

Long-term trending:

- Used to document the state of control of environmental conditions; establishes normal ("natural") variability
- Helps to evaluate the effectiveness of training, performance, cleaning methods, maintenance procedures, CAPA, and so on
- Used for weekly and monthly excursion trend analysis

The basic question when analyzing data for process trending purposes is: *Do you see any trend or pattern that deserves further investigation?*

Several common mistakes occur during trending analysis:

- We conclude that there is a trend when what we are "detecting" is the common variation present in all processes.
- We are unable to detect a real trend or pattern (We're trend blind; a common problem in the regulated industry).
- We fail to evaluate enough data points to cover normal variation of the process under analysis. (At least 15–20 are required.)

Verify whether the most recent data points are within expected range of variation. Do you see any pattern? Any daily, weekly, monthly, or seasonal trend?

Are SPC or control charts the correct tool for process trending?

Most of the processes in the life sciences regulated industry are not stable over long periods of time. For example, the critical quality attributes of a drug are most likely determined by the incoming materials used during manufacturing. As soon as we change the raw material, we can observe significant changes in the results of quality control tests. For this reason, typical control charts are not the best option to monitor those processes. A good substitute is the run chart, which is basically a control chart without limits:

- Both have the same purpose: to distinguish common from special-cause variation in the data produced by a process.
- Run charts originated from control charts, which were initially designed by Walter Shewhart.
- Run charts evolved from the development of these control charts, but run charts focus more on time patterns while a control chart focuses more on acceptable limits of the process.
- Run charts are simple to construct and to analyze and can be used with any process and any type of data.

Nonconformance investigations type 1 (see Table 4.4) must be evaluated periodically using a Pareto chart to focus on the most prevalent issues. Other available tools such as run charts or control charts are recommended to monitor the performance of the most significant processes and activities such as rework.

We do recommend a monthly review of the investigation and CAPA system trends. If, for some reason, this schedule is not feasible, review it bimonthly or quarterly. Less often than quarterly is not recommended.

Figure 4.6 is an example of monitoring of the scrap rate of a process. Baseline ranges from 2% to 3%, but something happened during December and the scrap rate rose to 7%. An investigation seems appropriate.

The book *Statistical Process Control for the FDA-Regulated Industry* published by ASQ Quality Press is an excellent reference for this topic of trending.[2]

4.2 PROBLEM INVESTIGATION: DISCOVERING ROOT CAUSES

Many investigation reports conclude that the root cause was some kind of *human error* or procedures not followed (by some human being) and immediately jump to solutions such as retraining. Most of the time these "solutions" are ineffective because they miss the principal and key element of the investigation and CAPA system: root causes.

Problems are best solved by identifying and eliminating root causes, as opposed to merely addressing the immediately obvious symptoms. By directing corrective actions at root causes, we hope that the probability of problem recurrence will be minimized. Root cause analysis is one of the most widely used approaches to problem solving and it is considered an iterative process, part of the continuous improvement tool collection.

Many times the problems are consequences of a combination of causes or, even worse, of the interaction of these causes. For this reason, a systematic approach to root cause analysis and problem solving is highly

[2] See Peña-Rodríguez, M. E. (2013).

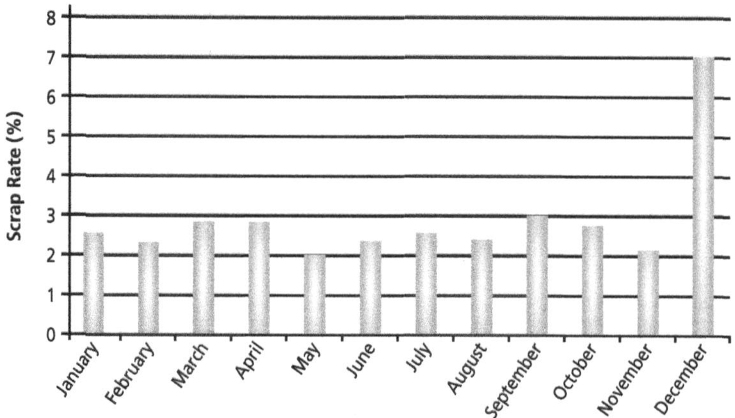

Figure 4.6 Scrap monthly rates.

recommended. The method and the tools to be used must be part of the investigation procedures. Making them requisites will ensure that your investigations are standardized enough and that they will enhance your overall investigation and CAPA system. Finally, but no less important, we should remember that most of the time root causes are directly linked to some weakness of the QMS.

4.2.1 Symptoms, Causal Factors, and Root Causes

When a company receives a customer complaint, or when a product fails its QC test, we are seeing only symptoms of some kind of problem. Problem symptoms and problem causes can look very much alike. For example, a broken piece of manufacturing equipment could be a symptom of poor maintenance, but it can also be the factor causing a product (manufactured with this equipment) to fail. This confusion between symptoms and true causes is especially dangerous in the case of the so-called human errors, which will be discussed in Chapter 5.

The symptom can be defined as the obvious or detectable manifestation of a causal factor, the condition (human error, equipment failure, or material failure) that directly caused the problem, allowed it to occur, or allowed the consequences to be worse. On the other hand, root causes are the basic reasons why causal factors occur or persist.

The main tool used to dig in this problem-solving process is a series of questions. Asking what, where, when, and how will help to identify causal factors that contribute to the problem. Asking why will help us to identify the root causes behind these causal factors. Figure 4.7 illustrates this process.

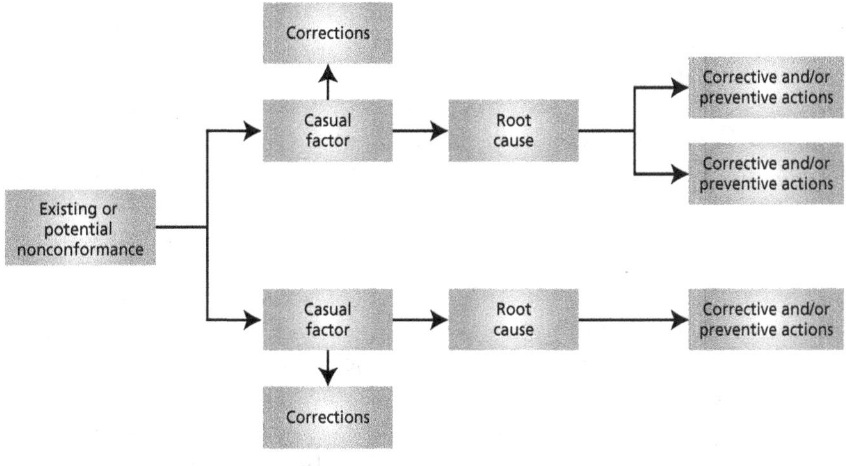

Figure 4.7 Root cause elements.

Starting with a symptom or detected problem (all the products stored inside the walk-in cooler at the distribution center were damaged), we should ask why that occurred. The answer has two parts: First, products were damaged because the refrigerator ceased to work during the weekend; second, the alarm that should have alerted security guards about the incident did not work. Both are obvious causal factors, not root causes. Many times, there is more than a single factor behind our problem and we should pursue all of them if we want to avoid the recurrence of the situation.

Many companies will stop at this point and determine that the only "corrective action" needed is to fix the broken piece of equipment and the alarm system. Both are merely corrections because they aim at the symptoms and not the root causes.

Taking the first factor, we must ask why the refrigerator's motor broke. We might learn that its maintenance schedule is too long (one year) and some motor components deteriorated earlier.

We can continue by asking why someone wrote that maintenance must be performed only once a year and then we must shorten that period, which will be a good corrective action. We know that the root cause is found when we are able to fix it. Simply repairing the motor does not guarantee that it will not fail again if it is not effectively maintained at the required intervals.

For the second causal factor (alarm not working), the question should be this: Why didn't it work? We learn that it was properly installed, but not included as part of the regular maintenance program. In this real case, no plant alarms were included in the scheduled maintenance. The fix to this root cause is also obvious: to include alarms in the maintenance procedure.

A classical technique regarding this topic is the use of the *5 Whys*. Must we always ask *why* five times? The answer is no. Looking at Figure 4.7, we see that each *why* will move us closer to the root causes. The first *why* moves us from the symptoms to their direct causal factors. Sometimes the second *why* finishes the work because it moves us to a fixable root cause. Other times, we must look at several layers of causal factors in order to discover the fixable root cause. The number of *whys* is not a fixed factor; it will depend on the issue under investigation. Experience tells us that five is more than sufficient in many cases.

For the purpose of a simple but robust investigation, the best use of resources might be to stop asking *why* when you reach a "fixable" root cause. In this example, some corrective actions could be (1) to shorten the maintenance interval for all the refrigerator motors to a more logical interval (you will need to justify the new period), and (2) to include all alarms in the maintenance program and procedure. The first corrective action can be extended as a preventive measure to other equipment having a long maintenance interval (first we must find them by performing a gap analysis of our maintenance program). The second preventive action should cover other equipment lacking maintenance in addition to the alarm.

Sometimes investigators try to fix world problems within a single investigation. Attempting to do so by continually asking *why* will often focus an investigation on corporate procedures and policies. (How does this company establish maintenance schedules?) That could slow the process and prevent approval of the investigation report within a reasonable period of time. I firmly believe that it is more than adequate to fix those root causes under our control (the ones described above) as soon as possible and let management analyze and decide the next level of action. This is exactly the requirement established by FDA and ISO 9001:2008. In the refrigerator example (see Figure 4.8), the management of the plant will periodically review relevant CAPA issues (for example, using a Pareto chart of root causes) and decide next steps. One decision could be to open a plant-wide or corporate CAPA to review the whole preventive maintenance program.

Table 4.5 shows several examples of symptoms, causal factors, and root causes. Table 4.6 includes some examples of two typical causal factors often mentioned as root causes on investigations from regulated industries.

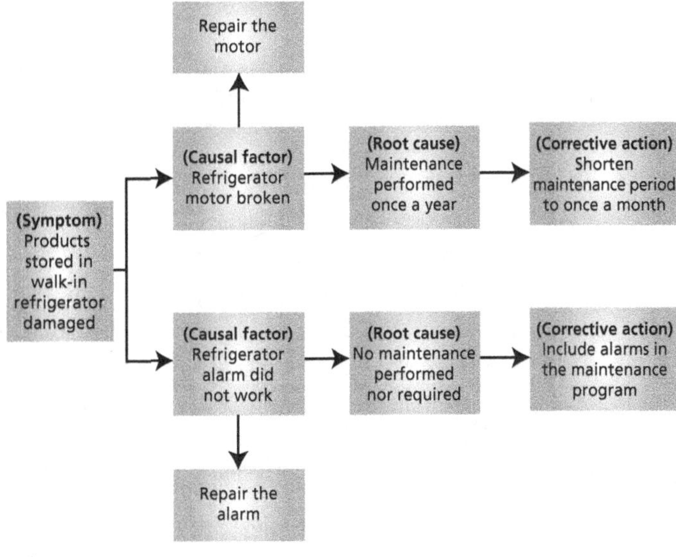

Figure 4.8 Investigation and CAPA example.

Table 4.5 Symptoms, causal factors, and root causes.

Symptoms	Causal factors	Root cause
Fever	Infected wound	Poor hygiene
Equipment broken	Not adequate maintenance or no maintenance at all	Procedure does not specify the maintenance or not include it
Product not homogeneous	Operator did not follow the mixing procedure	The procedure is ambiguous and it does not include sufficient details (for example, mix for a few seconds)
Incorrect information entered into the manufacturing record	Operator did not follow the procedure	Operator not properly trained because of training environment
Mathematical calculation mistakes (for example, rounding errors)	Human error	Operators were not properly trained on rounding numbers
Incorrect product label	Operators failed to detect the incorrect expiration date printed on the labels	Excessive load of work and an all-manual inspection activity

Table 4.6 Examples of causal factors and root causes.

Causal Factor	Root Causes
Human error or Procedure not followed	• Procedure not clear • Ambiguous or confusing instructions • Lack of sufficient details • Document format not adequate • Training instructor not adequate • Insufficient practice or hands-on experience • Frequency not adequate (insufficient refresher training) • Inattention to details • Lack of capabilities
Equipment failure	• Inadequate or defective design • Inadequate installation or validation • Historical lack of reliability • Equipment not included in the maintenance program • Corrective maintenance inadequate • Preventive maintenance inadequate

4.2.2 Fixing Symptoms: Corrections

Once you become aware of a nonconformance or deviation, the first actions should be to "stop the bleeding." Different names are used to describe this action: correction, remedial action, remedial corrections, containment action, and so on. In this book we use extensively *correction* to describe it.

Corrections are one of the three elements of the CAPA system along with corrective actions and preventive actions. Practically all nonconformances or deviations needs a correction. Even merely the concession to accept a nonconformity is technically a correction or remedial action. The main caution here is not to confuse a correction with a corrective action. The first one addresses the symptom; the second one should address the root cause(s) of the symptom.

Table 4.7 depicts some examples of corrections to better understand the concept.

Table 4.7 Symptoms and corrections.

Symptoms	Correction
Fever	Take antipyretic medicine
Equipment broken	Repair the equipment
Product not homogeneous	Make it homogeneous or discard (reject) it if rework is not possible/not allowed
Incorrect information entered into the manufacturing record	Enter the correct information Note: Depending on the circumstances, a simple note will be enough; in other cases, a formal nonconformance report will be need to sustain the correction
Wrong value used due to a mathematical calculation mistake	Use the correct value *Above note does apply here*
Incorrect product label	If the product is under our control, rework and place the correct label (if feasible) If product is distributed, a recall will be the adequate correction most of the time
Laboratory analysis gives an OOS	Place the batch on quarantine Once the OOS investigation is completed, possible outcome (and new corrections) may be: • reject and destroy the batch • invalidate the original OOS and re-test the batch
Stability testing failure	Place on quarantine any remaining inventory of the batch Unless the OOS result on the distributed batch is found to be invalid within three days, an initial FAR should be submitted (another correction) Once the stability OOS investigation is completed, if the failure is confirmed, the recall of the batch may be the necessary final correction
Customer complaint received pointing to potential problem with a batch	Place on quarantine any remain inventory Once the complaint investigation is completed, if nonconformance is confirmed the recall of the batch may be the necessary correction

In any case, always remember that corrections only fix symptoms. In addition to corrections, based on the significance of the problem and what your procedures say, you may need to perform an investigation to discover root cause(s) and then take appropriate corrective actions and/or preventive actions.

QC laboratory is a typical area where most of the time only corrections are provided in response to the frequent laboratory errors. Under an adequate quality system environment, laboratory error should be relatively rare. Frequent errors suggest a situation that might be due to inadequate training of analysts, poorly-maintained or improperly-calibrated equipment, or careless work. Whenever laboratory error (the symptom) is identified, the company should, at minimum, determine the source (root causes) of that error and take corrective action to avoid recurrence.

Table 4.8 describes the different CAPA system elements associated to a hypothetic laboratory "error" investigation.

4.2.3 Problem Description

The familiar expression "a problem well defined is a problem half solved" perfectly explains the reason for this section of the book. Very often the main reason for faulty CAPAs is the attempt to fix the problem as soon as possible without first understanding and clearly defining it.

Table 4.8 Typical laboratory error investigation.

Element	Action Performed
Symptom: Batch fails QC test (initial OOS investigation)	
Correction #1	Place the batch on quarantine
OOS initial investigation	Determine if the initial OOS was caused by a laboratory error or it was a true product failure An incorrect software configuration was discovered in the LIMS for this test. The incorrect configuration was uploaded during the last software update performed one week ago.
Correction #2	Invalidate initial OOS results and repeat the test using the correct software configuration
Root cause investigation	Determine which quality system control failures allowed the uploading of the incorrect configuration for this product
Corrective action	Modify existing controls or add new ones to avoid recurrence of incorrect software update for this product
Preventive action	Extend those controls to laboratory software used to test other products of this site/plant
Preventive action #2 (global)	Extend those controls to laboratory software used to test other products at other plants/sites of the company

During root cause analysis workshops, we ask participants to forget about the solution (corrective and preventive actions) and focus instead on the full understanding of the issue we are trying to solve. Skipping this crucial step limits us to implementing only spot fixes that address symptoms instead of taking adequate corrective or preventive actions aimed at root causes.

In other words, our problem-solving strategy must uncover root causes before we can determine the solution to the problem. We will use facts and data to narrow the search for the most probable root causes. We can conclude this introduction stating that if the problem is not clearly defined, completely and in detail, the problem cannot be solved!

We recommend the following four tools to describe/define the problem we are trying to solve:

- Flowchart—task analysis
- Chronology or timeline
- Change analysis
- Comparison matrix

Each tool includes references indicating where a detailed analysis can be found. A very good single reference book for quality tools is *The Quality Toolbox* by Nancy R. Tague.

Flowchart

A flowchart is a picture that describes the steps of a process in sequential order. It is useful when trying to understand how a process is really being done. Unfortunately, many companies do not have flowcharts of their processes. When trying to solve a problem, it is a good idea to spend some time walking through the process and comparing how things are actually done (the real process) with how they should be done (the theoretical process required by applicable working instructions). We especially recommend it when dealing with so-called human error; in this case, we can refer to it as a task analysis chart.

Chronology or Timeline

We recommend the use of a chronology or timeline. It can be defined as the arrangement of events in their order of occurrence. It must include a detailed description of events leading to the problem as well as those actions taken in reaction to the problem. Time is perhaps the most important element of any investigation because causal factors and root causes act on a specific and determined moment. Even if they seem to appear randomly, it is important to consider all pieces of information. The objective of this analysis is to determine when the problem began.

Ordering the facts of an investigation by time has two main purposes:

- It helps you understand the problem.
- It helps you write the investigation report.

During our workshops, participants work with case studies containing dozens of facts and dates. When completing the chronology analysis, most of them ignore at least half of those dates. Ordering the facts by time is often the only tool you need to discover the key path to the root cause. In the real example in Figure 4.9, it was noticed that the problem appeared (a sharp increase in the laboratory result variability) right after major maintenance work was performed in the facilities. Unsupervised maintenance workers moved calibrated balances and other laboratory equipment in order to perform their duties and then replaced them. The first and only apparent sign of these movements was that high variation.

Change Analysis

This tool helps to identify relevant changes in the process that may lead to the root cause of our problem. We can perform a change-point analysis to determine whether a change occurred, identify the moment of that change, and finally determine whether multiple changes have occurred. Most new (non-chronic) problems start with some kind of change, either new materials or components, new process, new people, or new specifications. The basic idea is to ask what may have changed prior to the detection of the problem.

In the example described in Figure 4.10, the graph clearly helps to identify that this company had two surges in customer complaints during the past year. The manufacturing dates of the faulty products align almost exactly with two situations where new operators were incorporated. Based on this information, the investigation focused on the evaluation of training received by these new hires. You can imagine the root cause.

Stratification or data segregation is a data analysis tool recommended when data from a variety of sources have been combined. In such a situation, it can be difficult to detect the meaning of the data. Data coming from several sources or conditions (such as shifts, machines, days of the week, or different suppliers) should be submitted to this analysis.

The stratification analysis can be performed graphically (scatter diagram, control chart, histogram, or other graphical analysis tool) by assigning different marks or colors to distinguish data from different sources. It can be statistically performed by using ANOVA. Data that are distinguished in this way are said to be "stratified." A typical use is to analyze productivity by machine to see whether we can identify any pattern.

Date (week of)	Facts
Oct 12th	Results within specifications
Oct 19th	Floor maintenance housekeeping performed during the weekend
Oct 26th	High variability of results. The two balances were found out of tolerance. Balances were calibrated.
Nov 2nd	Results within specifications
Nov 9th	Results within specifications
Nov 16th	Results within specifications
Nov 23rd	Results within specifications
Nov 30th	Results within specifications
Dec 7th	Results within specifications
Dec 14th	Floor maintenance housekeeping performed during the weekend
Dec 21st	High variability of results. The two balances were found out of tolerance. Balances were calibrated.
Dec 28th	Results within specifications

Figure 4.9 Timeline of event.

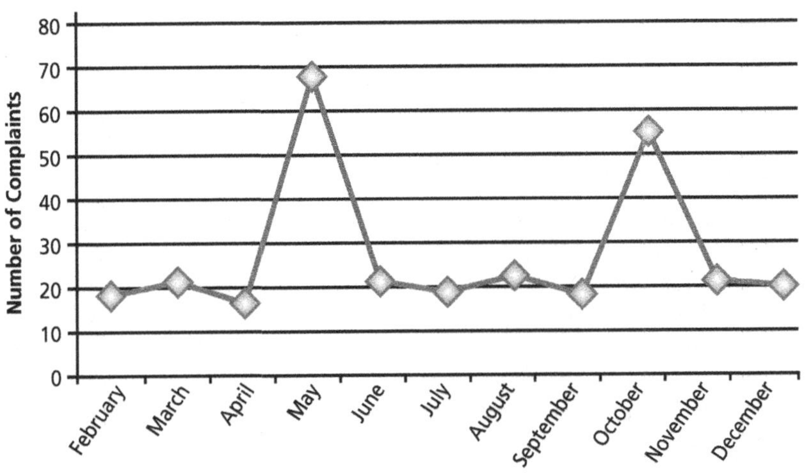

Figure 4.10 Change analysis graph.

Comparison Matrix

The primary name of this tool is the Is-Is Not matrix. It is also called the K–T diagram in honor of problem-solving pioneers Dr. Charles Kepner and Dr. Benjamin Tregoe. It guides the search for causes of a problem or undesirable situation. By comparing *what, when, where,* and the *extent* of our problem (the *Is*) with *what else, where else, when else* and *to what other extent* the problem might have reasonably been (the *Is Not*), we can see what is distinctive about this problem and this leads us to potential root causes. The comparison matrix complements the change analysis tool previously discussed.

We prefer the use of the word *comparison* to name this tool because many companies are using a variation of it that simply describes *what is* and *what is not* the problem without performing the critical comparison work, which is where the real value of this tool lays.

The final outcome of this comparison matrix is three paragraphs. The first describes the problem in detail. The second paragraph describes *what is not* the problem (but could have been). The third and most important paragraph describes the distinctions between each *Is* and *Is Not* pair (what is different, odd, special, or unusual about them).

The best way to use this tool is to hand it over to a cross-functional team. Typically, the team encounters more difficulty trying to complete the *Is Not* column than the *Is* information. At times, due to the unique nature of some issues, the *Is Not* section cannot be completed for a specific characteristic. In this situation obviously no comparison can be made for such specific item of the matrix.

Very often, the information gathered at this stage of the problem-solving process is the base for the cause-and-effect diagram or the fault tree analysis tools described in the next section. Once we arrive at the root cause, it can be tested against the comparison matrix facts to see how well it fits.

4.2.4 Barrier Analysis

Control barrier analysis is the evaluation of current process controls to determine whether all the current barriers pertaining to the problem you are investigating were present and effective (even if they worked or not). The origin of this concept relates to the safety field where the term "barrier" is used to mean any barrier, defense, or control that is in place to increase the safety of a system. Barrier analysis can be used both proactively (for example performing a risk assessment using FMEA) or retrospectively (for example to perform a *post-mortem* incident analysis using fault three analysis). There are two main types of barriers: physical and administrative. Physical barriers are the most reliable in terms of providing failsafe solutions to problems. Administrative barriers are considered to be least reliable barriers, in terms of failsafe, because they

Table 4.9 Barrier controls.

Physical and Natural Barriers	Administrative Barriers
• Separation among manufacturing or packaging lines • Emergency power supply • Dedicated equipment • Barcoding • Keypad controlled doors • Separated storage for components • Software which prevents to going further if a field is not completed • Redundant designs	• Training and certifications • Clear procedures and policies • Adequate supervision • Adequate load of work • Use of checklist • Verification of critical task by a second person • Periodic process audits

rely on human action and behavior. Examples of each type of control barrier are included in the Table 4.9.

It is very important to understand that for most of the "typical" human errors (topic extensively covered in Chapter 5), barriers trying to minimize the impact of the potential errors are the *best option* we have to make our process more robust. As important as answering to *why that happened*? is to respond *why did we not detect it earlier*?

Table 4.10 depicts an example of a typical situation where a pharmaceutical product reached the market with incorrect information on its label although as many as four barrier controls were in place. Why did they fail? An egregious example of this situation was a product recalled because its label stated an expiration date of 07/2104 instead of 07/2014.

Table 4.10 Barrier control analysis example.

Problem	Current controls	Current controls evaluation Why they failed?
Incorrect expiration date on label	Line clearance	Item not specifically included in the line clearance
	In-process manufacturing inspection	No formal checklist for inspection
	Final manufacturing inspection	No formal checklist for final manufacturing inspection
	Final quality product release	No formal checklist for final quality inspection

4.2.5 Root Cause Identification Processes and Tools

Once we have a well-defined problem with sufficient facts and data, the next step will be the identification of all possible causes at the origin of the problem. Moving from the causal factors that directly created the symptoms to the true root causes very often requires the use of a disciplined approach including standard tools to identify root causes. It also benefits from creativity, good data collection, and objective and analytical reasoning.

Many of the chronic and persistent problems we face within the regulated industry are not the direct result of a single root cause. Many times, they result from a combination of causes or, even worse, from the interaction of causes. This is one of the basic reasons why the classic trial-and-error methodology of problem solving does not work most of the time. It could be acceptable just to fix the problem if you are working in other less regulated environments. For the regulated field, we must effectively fix root causes, verify that the actions already taken have worked, and generate a documentation trail covering all the phases of the problem-solving exercise.

4.2.5.1 The Investigation Plan

The investigation plan is probably the most important element of your investigation. An investigation is:

- A systematic process of collecting relevant evidence; followed by
- An assessment of the evidence gathered; followed by
- A logical and reasonable determination or conclusion.

To be meaningful, the investigation should be thorough, timely, unbiased, well-documented, and scientifically sound. The investigator (alone or as a member of an investigating team) is responsible for gathering all the relevant evidence or information and then using this to find the facts. But an investigation is not a trial. You are not a prosecutor or plaintiff, but an impartial fact-gatherer. You have a duty both to collect the information and to assess it. At the end of the process you must report your findings in an independent and objective way.

Planning is essential to ensure that:

- The investigation is carried out methodically and in a professional manner
- Resources are used efficiently
- The focus is maintained; you are not going back and forth or employing trial and error as you look for causes
- Additional resources (for example, subject matter experts) can be made available if required
- Potential root causes are not overlooked

The main (and best) planning tool available to an investigator is an **investigation plan**. There are a number of ways in which you may develop an investigation plan. While it is important that you start with a plan, investigations rarely proceed as originally predicted. You should therefore be ready to revise your plan, perhaps drastically, as new information emerges during the course of an investigation. Always follow the facts, rather than trying to make the facts fit into your plan. An investigation plan will define what you do, why you do it and when you do it. It should include at minimum the following elements:

a. A clear statement of the reason for the investigation.

b. A summary of the factors (potential causes) of the process that may have caused the problem

c. The type of documentation review will be performed, including the time frame for such historical data evaluation

d. If the investigation plan includes performing additional tests, a protocol should be prepared (subject to approval by the quality area) that describes the additional testing to be performed and specifies the scientific and/or technical handling of the data. This is particularly important if your plan requires any test to material already on the market.

Sometimes, it is particularly important to decide, as part of the investigation plan, if we are going to perform one investigation or we should split the issue we are handling into more than one investigation. A couple of examples may help to clarify this.

> Case 1: One batch of tablets failed an analytical test (potency out-of-specification) and it also failed the appearance test due to the presence of black specks. These seem to be clearly two unconnected problems affecting the same batch. We will recommend generating two separate investigation reports, one for each situation. If you decide to investigate both situations under the same report, then you'll need to be very careful to assure you work with both issues simultaneously, including two different investigation plans. You'll end with two investigations under the same report anyway, hence our recommendation to split them from the onset and handle them independently.

> Case 2: Two batches of the same product failed the same test back to back. We recommend you to combine both issues under one investigation report and include both under the same investigation plan.

4.2.5.2 Root Cause Identification Tools

We have seen many regulated companies spend a lot of money on problem-solving training and still have a very poor investigation and CAPA system. While auditing their investigation and CAPA procedures, one can easily see the reason: a lot of *should be* and *can be* ("fishbone, fault tree, or any other problem-solving technique can be used") instead of *must be* ("fishbone must be included on every investigation").

The best recommendation we can provide to regulated companies is to require (not simply recommend) the use of selected tools. We recommend the following four tools as requirements for any root cause investigation:

- Chronology
- Comparison matrix
- Cause-and-effect diagram
- Fault tree analysis

We have not seen a single case where the use of those quality tools has damaged the root cause analysis process. With some training, an average investigator can complete them in a reasonable period of time. Chronology and comparison matrix were discussed on chapter 4.2.3.

Cause-and-Effect Diagram

Cause and effect diagrams (Ishikawa diagram) are used to analyze and find the root cause of a certain effect or problem. These are also known as fishbone diagrams because their shape is similar to that of a fish skeleton. Fishbone diagrams are considered one of the seven basic tools of quality management.

The fishbone diagram focuses on the causes rather than the effect. Because there may be a number of causes for a particular problem, this tool helps us to identify the root cause of the problem in an uncomplicated manner. This tool allows brainstorming in a structured format similar to an affinity diagram, where potential causes are grouped into logical categories such as materials, manpower, methods, machines, environment, and so on.

Potential causes can be further tracked back to the root cause using the *5 Whys* technique. Another way to do this is to examine the problem using typical categories known as the 5 Ms and 1 E:

- Manpower: Anyone involved with the process
- Methods: How the process is performed and the specific requirements for doing it, such as policies, procedures, instructions, and regulations
- Machines: Any equipment, computers, or tools required to accomplish the task

- Materials: Raw materials, parts, and components used to produce the final product
- Measurements: Data generated from the process that are used to evaluate it
- Environment: Environmental conditions such as humidity and temperature and the culture in which the process operates

In addition to using the fishbone diagram (or a table containing the categories and potential causes), it is recommended to include a detailed discussion of each category as part of your investigation report. Do not simply document the most probable cause based on your analysis. You must always include in your discussion the reason why you discarded or ruled out most of the identified potential causes and what objective evidence you have to support your selection of the root causes or most probable root causes. Chapter 8.4.2 includes a detailed root cause analysis checklist using the causes described in Chapter 4.2.6.

Fault Tree Analysis

Fault tree analysis (FTA) is a type of analysis in which a failure is analyzed using Boolean logic to combine a series of lower-level events (causal factors) until we reach their root causes. This analysis method was originally developed to quantitatively determine the probability of a safety hazard in the field of safety engineering.

Fault tree analysis provides a method of breaking down chains of failures, and permits the identification of combinations or interactions of events that cause other failure events. There are two types of interaction:

1. Several items must fail together to cause another item to fail ("AND" combination)
2. Only one of a number of possible events must happen to cause another item to fail ("OR" combination)

The "AND" and "OR" are called *gates*. They prevent the failure event above them to occur unless their specific conditions are met. When several factors must happen simultaneously ("AND" relationship), we can avoid the failure simply by controlling one of them (the easiest or the cheapest). When any of several causal factors can create the failure, then we must fix all of them. (See the fire example in Figure 4.11.)

The tree is constructed working backward from a known event or failure and asking why it happened. The answer will represent the factor that directly caused the failure. Continuing with the *why* questioning will allow us to reach fundamental events or root causes. In other words, the FTA is a very good tool to help us understand how an event occurred. It is best used when working with complex issues with several interrelated causes of failure.

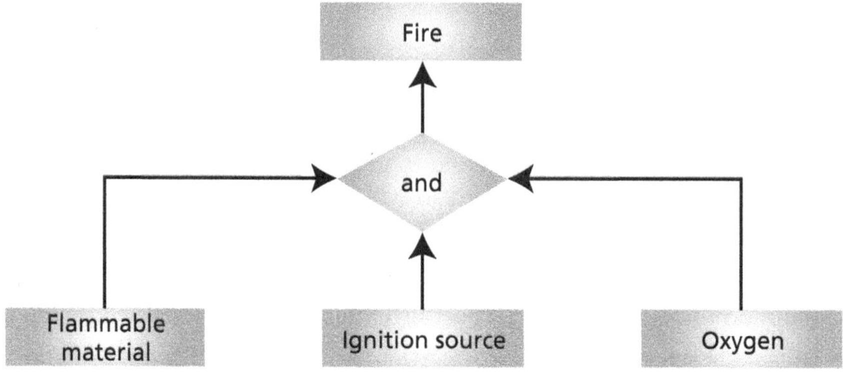

Figure 4.11 Fault tree analysis example.

FTA is a deductive, top-down approach to failure mode analysis aimed at analyzing the possible causes of an undesired event or failure. This contrasts with failure mode and effect analysis (FMEA), an inductive, bottom-up analysis method aimed at analyzing the effects of single-component or function failures on equipment or systems.

In terms of the investigation and CAPA system, we can define FTA as a reactive investigation tool (the failure already happened). FMEA should, ideally, be used proactively (during the design phase of a process) to anticipate failure modes and generate preventive actions.

For a detailed description and examples of this tool, see Tague (2005).

A Few Words about the 5 Whys

One of the most repeated words in the past few pages is *why*. As an investigator, you are searching for the true causes of your problems. If you don't know the cause, you cannot implement corrective action. Remember the definition of corrective action: action to avoid the recurrence of root causes. There are plenty of root cause analysis tools available to you; most of them are more complicated to understand than your own problem, but all of them are based on the word *why*.

The best way to find your path from the symptoms to the root causes is to ask *why* until the nature of your problem and its solution become clear. This tool (the *5 Whys*) is attributed to one of the founders of the Toyota Company (Sakichi Toyoda).

Why five? It is postulated that five iterations are generally sufficient to get to a root cause. My recommendation is that you keep asking *why* until a fixable root cause is found.

Once You Have Found the Root Cause or Causes of Your Problem

Another possible outcome of the root cause investigation is that sometimes you will arrive nowhere. If you cannot find the root cause, you will be unable to develop corrective action. In this situation you must be sure to generate a complete investigation report demonstrating the problem-solving work performed. Any educated reviewer of your report must be able to conclude that your inability to find the root cause was not the result of a poor investigation. Be sure to look for potential root causes that you can address through preventive actions. After all, without corrective actions, those preventive actions are all you can do to improve your process.

If you perform a methodical investigation, most of the time you will discover fixable root causes related to the situation you are working on. When several causes are identified, all of them must be addressed within the CAPA plan. Failing to do that is one of the biggest opportunities of the CAPA system as discussed in Chapter 6.

4.2.6 Root Cause Categories

Trending of root cause categories is one of the most critical metrics management must periodically evaluate. To help with this process, we offer a list we have been developing for years that includes more than 60 categories. The list is also provided as a template in section 8.4.2, including a column to document the rationale to rule-in or rule-out each root cause. It can help to reinforce your investigation and CAPA system in several ways:

- Increase consistency across all investigations
- Facilitate consistency across the organization
- Allow trending of categories and root causes

The root cause list *is not* meant to be used for picking a cause without the proper root cause analysis process. This list is not static and can be modified to include new categories. However, resist the temptation to create an "other" category. You are likely to finish with most of the root causes classified as "other" and this defeats the purpose of the list.

Once you arrive at the root cause, try to confirm it. If possible and practical, conduct a controlled experiment to verify that the root cause effectively creates the symptoms you detected.

1. **Personal Performance**
   - 1.1 Lack of attention (inattention to details, working from memory)
   - 1.2 Continuous attitude problems
   - 1.3 Fatigue

- 1.4 Lack of capability (sensory, physical, intellectual)
- 1.5 Personal problems
- 1.6 Medication problems

2. Training

- 2.1 Lack of training
  - 2.1.1 Training not required
  - 2.1.2 Missing training
- 2.2 Training not effective
  - 2.2.1 Content not adequate (task analysis, qualification/certification)
  - 2.2.2 Training method not adequate
  - 2.2.3 Language barriers
  - 2.2.4 Environment not adequate
  - 2.2.5 Instructor not adequate
  - 2.2.6 Insufficient practice or hands-on experience
  - 2.2.7 Frequency not adequate (insufficient refresher training)

3. Equipment

- 3.1 Design and/or installation
  - 3.1.1 Inadequate or defective design
  - 3.1.2 Inadequate installation or validation
- 3.2 Equipment reliability
  - 3.2.1 Historical lack of reliability
- 3.3 Equipment maintenance
  - 3.3.1 Equipment not included in the maintenance program
  - 3.3.2 Inadequate corrective maintenance
  - 3.3.3 Inadequate preventive maintenance
- 3.4 Calibration issues
  - 3.4.1 Equipment not calibrated
  - 3.4.2 Calibration failure
  - 3.4.3 Missing equipment
- 3.5 Utilization of the equipment
  - 3.5.1 Incorrect utilization of the equipment

4. Human Reliability Factors

4.1 Work area

4.1.1 Inadequate location of equipment

4.1.2 Inadequate identification of equipment, materials

4.1.3 Cluttered or inadequate layout

4.2 Work environment

4.2.1 Uncomfortable environment conditions (cold, hot, poor illumination)

4.2.2 Inadequate housekeeping

4.2.3 Stress conditions (rush)

4.3 Work load

4.3.1 Excessive work load

4.3.2 Excessive calculation or data manipulation

4.3.3 Multitasking

5. Procedures and Instructions / Task Design

5.1 Not used

5.1.1 Lack of procedure or instruction

5.1.2 Not required

5.1.3 Not available or difficult to obtain

5.1.4 Difficult to use

5.1.5 Decision not to use / follow document

5.2 Misleading or confusing

5.2.1 Ambiguous or confusing instructions

5.2.2 Lack of sufficient details

5.2.3 Document format not adequate

5.3 Wrong or incomplete

5.3.1 Incomplete instructions

5.3.2 Wrong instruction

5.3.3 Typographical error(s)

5.4 Obsolete

5.4.1 Obsolete document

5.5 Not approved

5.5.1 Document not approved

6. **Materials**
   - 6.1 Material controls
     - 6.1.1 Inadequate storage conditions
     - 6.1.2 Inadequate sampling instructions
     - 6.1.3 Material not adequate (hold / quarantined)
     - 6.1.4 Inadequate material substitution
     - 6.1.5 Shipping damage
     - 6.1.6 Marginal material
   - 6.2 Purchasing control
     - 6.2.1 Specification not appropriate
     - 6.2.2 Marginal supplier
     - 6.2.3 Supplier not approved
7. **Environment**
   - 7.1 Inadequate pest control
   - 7.2 Unfavorable ambient conditions
8. **Supervision and Management Factors**
   - 8.1 Verbal instructions / communication problem
   - 8.2 Inadequate communication between shifts
   - 8.3 Inadequate supervision
   - 8.4 Improper resources allocation (lack of personnel)

4.3 CAPA PLAN: CORRECTIVE AND PREVENTIVE ACTIONS TO FIX ROOT CAUSES

Once we arrive at the probable causes behind our problems, it is time to develop an effective plan to avoid the recurrence of those causes. The best root cause investigation is worthless if the identified causes are not addressed. These plans must cover the following four sequential elements:

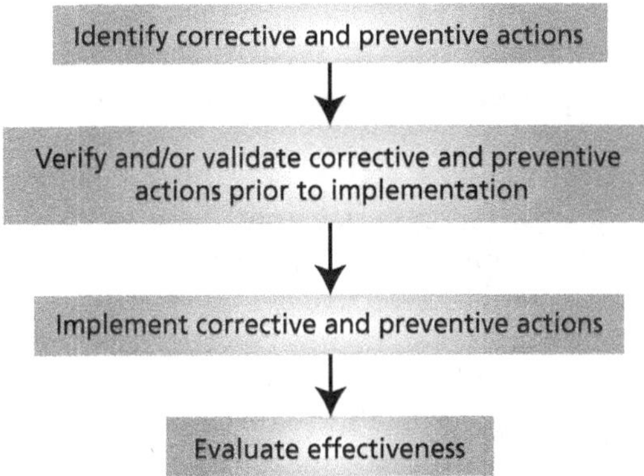

The elaboration of an adequate CAPA plan requires time. Most companies do not recognize this, which is one of the main reasons why most CAPA systems are ineffective. One or two weeks seems to be an adequate period in which to decide the most effective way to address the identified root causes. During this time the investigator can evaluate where else the actions can be applied. If the corrective action is to clarify document X, the common inadequate preventive action would be to evaluate whether other documents must be clarified. The correct approach must be to perform such evaluation during the one- or two-week period described above and then write the preventive action as "clarify documents Y and Z," which were found with the same kind of problem. *Analyze, evaluate, assess,* and so on are not adequate corrective or preventive actions.

4.3.1 Establish Effective Corrective and Preventive Actions

For each root cause identified, we must generate an adequate corrective and/or preventive action. Section 1.4 has a detailed discussion of corrective versus preventive. The key point is that the investigator must be sure that every identified root cause is covered in the CAPA plan. Many times there are several root causes, but corrective actions address only one of them.

Another gray area of responsibility has to do with who should prepare the CAPA plan. The CAPA plan encompasses the identification of corrective and/or preventive actions, their verification and/or validation (prior to implementation), their implementation, and finally the evaluation of the plan's effectiveness. Usually the person best positioned to prepare a good CAPA plan is the owner of the process or system that needs to be fixed. The CAPA plan must be a team effort including subject matter experts as well as the investigator or someone from the investigation team. Section 8.4.4 includes examples of CAPA plans.

Each corrective or preventive action included in the CAPA plan must include a detailed description of every single action to be taken and an explanation of how the action will avoid the recurrence (or occurrence, if working with a preventive action) of the identified root cause. The plan must also include a description of how the action will be validated or verified, as well as details about its implementation (when and by whom). If the implementation is not immediate (something common in our industry), some *interim* actions must be included to minimize the risk of recurrence while the corrective action is implemented. Finally, for each corrective action we must always consider whether that action can be extended to other products/processes/systems not yet affected by this root cause. If the answer is affirmative, a preventive action must be created to prevent the same cause from acting elsewhere.

If you have root causes that already occurred, you must have corrective actions. If you can extend the corrective actions to other places, then you will also have some preventive actions. On the other hand, if you only have potential root causes, you cannot have corrective actions; therefore, only preventive actions can be implemented.

4.3.2 Validation and Verification Prior to Implementation

Once the team decides how to fix the identified root causes, it must make sure that the proposed corrective and/or preventive actions will work, and achieve the desired results from implementation. The medical device regulation includes this requirement under §820.100(a)(4) says, "Verifying or validating the corrective and preventive action to ensure that such action is effective and does not adversely affect the finished device." Simply stated, you do not want the cure to be worse than the disease. Comment 163 of the medical devices regulation preamble states that "preventive, as well as corrective, action must be verified or validated" and remarks that "this definition makes the regulation consistent with ISO 9001:1994."

In simple terms, we can say that there is a lot of confusion with the meaning of this section of the regulation. Remember that the medical devices regulation is considered the gold standard for CAPA. A number of companies interpret this section to require evaluation of the effectiveness of all corrective actions *prior* to implementation, which is impossible.

If the corrective or preventive action does affect any validated item (for example, a validated test method, a validated piece of equipment, or a validated process) then we must perform some validation work in order to secure permission to implement the action. Do not perform a validation simply because it is a corrective or preventive action; validate because your procedures and your quality system require that such action must be performed prior to implementation.

If the preventive action is to change the current visual inspection to a sophisticated electronic inspection, we must validate the inspection device to ensure that the new inspection process will consistently produce a result that meets its predetermined specifications. In this specific case, it means that the electronic eye will detect nonconformances with a predetermined confidence level.

On the other hand, if the corrective or preventive action consists merely of a clarification of some written instruction, without a major change to a process, then a validation is not necessary. The document will be changed through a formal change control process that establishes who can change the document, who must approve it, and what training requirements are associated to it. This rigorous control of the proposed change can be considered the *verification* of the adequacy of the change.

As part of the justification for the implementation, you must also discuss why the proposed change will not produce adverse effects on the product. If you decide to change a component, several kind of studies will be needed prior to its implementation depending upon the product (stability, biocompatibility, and so on).

When a proposed action affects the design of medical devices, some design verification and/or validation work may be required. FDA regulation also requires that all software changes shall be validated. The FDA's analysis of 3140 medical device recalls conducted between 1992 and 1998 reveals that 242 of them (7.7 percent) were attributable to software failures. Of those software-related recalls, 192 (or 79 percent) were caused by software defects introduced when changes were made to the software after its initial production and distribution. Software validation and other related good software engineering practices discussed in this guidance are a principal means of avoiding such defects and resultant recalls.[3] Therefore, the CAPA plan document must include:

- Description of the actions to be taken
- When it will be implemented and who is responsible for that implementation
- Effectiveness evaluation: how, when, and by whom

4.3.3 Implementation of Corrective and Preventive Actions

A frequent observation issued by FDA inspectors is that corrective and preventive actions were not implemented. To avoid this embarrassing problem, every regulated company needs a clear accountability of responsibilities as well as an adequate tracking system to verify the implementation of each corrective or preventive action.

[3] General Principles of Software Validation; Final Guidance for Industry and FDA Staff (2002).

4.4 EFFECTIVENESS EVALUATION

4.4.1 Verifying That Solutions Worked

Finally, it is time to determine the effectiveness of corrective or preventive actions. Talking in terms of problems and solutions, we must verify that the solutions worked. Two main elements here are *how* and *when* the verification is accomplished.

One of my favorite things to do at the beginning of a CAPA training session is to ask participants what and how the effectiveness of implemented actions is evaluated. Most participants mention that an action is effective if the problem does not recur. Rarely someone defines it correctly as the lack of recurrence of the root causes. Once we define what a corrective or preventive action is (the action that addresses the root cause), everyone understands that the effectiveness relates to causes, not to symptoms or problems.

If similar symptoms are observed, do not jump to the conclusion that the action was not effective. To be able to conclude this, you must first identify the root causes of this repeated symptom. If you reach the same cause, then you can conclude that the previous action was ineffective. If you discover that this time the problem was the result of a different root cause (a common situation), then the effectiveness of your previous action is not in question. Within the same line of reasoning, sometimes you investigate a new problem and discover that the situation was created by a root cause you already fixed. In this case, you have evidence that the previous corrective or preventive action was not effective.

There are also some misunderstandings related to effectiveness verification. Some companies document that the action was implemented and not whether the action worked. If the action is not implemented, it does not have a chance to be effective; the implementation verification (discussed in the previous section) is a different concept. At this point of the CAPA cycle, the quality system asks for evidence that the implemented corrective or preventive action was effective and that the intended objective was accomplished.

Root causes are detected through the symptoms they produce. Therefore, the way to determine whether a corrective action was effective is to analyze the process that root cause acted upon. A typical question here is how long it takes to verify the effectiveness of the actions. Some companies have a fixed period of time (three months, six months, or one year); others take a more correct approach by linking that period of time to the frequency of the process being fixed.

A rule of thumb we recommend using is the "double digit" rule. It requires having at least ten repetitions of the process where the corrective or preventive action was applied prior to establishing whether the action was effective. If we use a fixed period (for example three months) and the process is performed monthly, we will have only three results (in the best case) to determine such effectiveness. Statistically there is a large probability that those first three repetitions are OK simply by chance even though the action did not work. By extending the evaluation to at least 10 repetitions, we increase our confidence level. With 10 good results, we can be confident that the action worked.

The documentation of the effectiveness evaluation should be generated along with the rest of the CAPA plan. Once we document the implementation of the action, the only remaining (open) task from the plan will be the effectiveness evaluation. The vast majority of CAPA effectiveness plans are totally reactive. We always recommend establishing a verification method that proactively looks for measures of effectiveness. A typical situation can be the implementation of a corrective action after we receive several complaints for a product. In this scenario, the action will be considered effective if no complaints are received during the next three months. Lack of complaints do not necessarily mean that we fixed the issue. A more adequate way to determine the effectiveness of the corrective action can be to monitor the next five or ten batches produced using an appropriate sampling plan. This statistically sound sampling plan can provide an adequate confidence level about the effectiveness of the action. And yes, it is fine it you also include as a second element of this effectiveness verification some criterion regarding a reduction in customer complaints associated to this root cause.

Chapter 8.6 includes several examples of effectiveness evaluation methods as part of the CAPA plan examples.

4.4.2 Training Effectiveness

Training is a critical component in any organization's strategy, but regulated companies rarely evaluate the impact of their training programs. *The management of effective training* provides the overall structure needed to ensure that training programs have processes in place to support regulated operations. Organizations that monitor training effectiveness and strive to improve weaknesses are consistently the best performers. It is important to develop methodologies to measure, evaluate, and continuously improve training.

Very often, the training function is seen as an expenditure center rather than as one of the most critical activities in any organization, especially in highly-regulated environments such as nuclear, aerospace, medical, and pharmaceutical. In these industries, training results must be measured. Incorporating selected training metrics into a reporting strategy can help demonstrate the real value of training. Measurements that consider performance improvements can provide a benchmark for training effectiveness.

A very important consideration is that most of the corrective or preventive actions are related with some training efforts, and therefore the effectiveness of these training actions must be evaluated. However, for most companies the only record generated from training activities is the attendance sheet itself. When evaluating the possible impact of training during nonconformance investigations, these sheets merely determine whether the personnel involved in the failure signed the corresponding training roster. If so, they conclude that training can be discarded as a root cause of the situation. Training effectiveness is not an explicit requirement of FDA regulations, but the FDA has expectations regarding these topics that are included in several guidance documents. The Agency's expectation is that firms must evaluate the effectiveness of their personnel training because it is a direct indicator of the robustness of the firm's quality system.

Quality data (complaints, failure investigations, audits, record reviews, and so on) must be used to assess both training needs and effectiveness. Human errors must be detected, trended, investigated, and corrected. Do not use retraining as a corrective action.

The FDA Guidance for Industry: Quality Systems Approach to Pharmaceutical CGMP Regulations states that "under a quality system, managers are expected to establish training programs that include the following:

- *Evaluation of training needs*
- *Provision of training to satisfy these needs*
- *Evaluation of effectiveness of training*
- *Documentation of training and/or re-training"*

The new standard ISO 9001:2015 includes under clause 7.2. (Competence) that the organization shall:

a. *determine the necessary competence of person(s) doing work under its control that affect the performance and effectiveness of the quality management system;*

b. *ensure that these persons are competent on the basis of appropriate education, training, or experience;*

c. *where applicable, take actions to acquire the necessary competence, and evaluate the effectiveness of the actions taken;*

d. *retain appropriate documented information as evidence of competence.*

Evaluation of effectiveness of training is also a requirement of ISO 13485:2003 and it is part of most of the foreign regulations pertaining to this type of industry. As if we need more reasons for the evaluation of training, here are a few others:

- To justify the existence and budget of the training department by showing how it contributes to the organization's objectives and goals
- To decide whether to continue or discontinue specific training programs
- To gain information on how to improve future training programs
  - Physical facilities, schedule, materials, food, material contents, instructors, and so on

The Kirkpatrick Model for Training Effectiveness Evaluation

More than half a century ago, Donald L. Kirkpatrick introduced a four-step approach to training evaluation. His four steps have become commonly known in the training field as Level One, Level Two, Level Three, and Level Four Evaluation. Table 4.12 reflects these four levels of evaluation.

Level One: Reaction

Kirkpatrick defines this first level of evaluation as determining "how well trainees liked a particular training program," "measuring the feelings of trainees," or "measuring the customer satisfaction." He outlines the following guidelines for evaluating reaction:

1. Determine what you want to learn.
2. Use a written comment sheet covering those items determined in Step 1.
3. Design the form so that reactions can be tabulated and quantified.
4. Obtain honest reactions by making the forms anonymous.
5. Encourage the trainees to write additional comments not covered by questions that were designed to be tabulated and quantified.

Table 4.12 The four levels of the Kirkpatrick Model.

Level	What	When
Reaction	Did they like it?	Upon completion of the training
Learning	Did they learn it?	Before and after training
Behavior	Did they use it?	Before and after training
Results	Did they produce measurable positive business results?	Before and after training

Kirkpatrick also suggests measuring the reaction of the training managers and other qualified observers. An analysis of these two groups would give the best indication of the effectiveness of the program at this first level of training evaluation.

Level Two: Learning

Kirkpatrick defines learning as "attitudes that were changed, and knowledge and skills that were learned." He outlines the following guidelines to evaluate learning:

1. The learning of each trainee should be measured so that quantitative results can be determined.
2. A before-and-after approach should be used so that any learning can be related to the program.
3. Where practical, a control group not receiving the training should be compared with the group that received the training.
4. Where practical, the evaluation results should be analyzed statistically so that learning can be proved in terms of correlation or level of confidence.

In addition to using written and oral examinations and performance tests, Kirkpatrick suggests that if a program is carefully designed, learning can be fairly and objectively evaluated while the training session is being conducted. For example, individual performance of a skill being taught and discussions following a role-playing situation can be used as evaluation techniques.

Level Three: Behavior (the Transfer of Training)

Realizing that "there may be a big difference between knowing principles and techniques and using them on the job," Kirkpatrick suggests that the following five requirements must be met for change in behavior to occur:

1. Desire to change
2. Knowledge of what to do and how to do it
3. The right job climate
4. Help in applying what was learned during training
5. Rewards for changing behavior

Kirkpatrick outlines the following guidelines for evaluating training programs in terms of behavioral changes on the job:

1. A systematic appraisal should be made of on-the-job performance on a *before-and-after* basis.
2. The appraisal of performance should be made by one or more of the following groups (the more the better):
   - The person receiving the training,
   - The person's supervisor,
   - The person's subordinates (if any),
   - The person's peers or other people thoroughly familiar with his or her performance.
3. A statistical analysis should be made to compare performance before and after and to relate changes to the training program.
4. The post-training appraisal should be made three months or more after the training so that the trainees have an opportunity to put into practice what they have learned. Subsequent appraisals may add to the validity of the study.
5. A control group (not receiving the training) should be used.

Kirkpatrick establishes that "measuring changes in behavior resulting from training programs involves a very complicated procedure." Nevertheless, it is worthwhile if training programs are to increase in effectiveness and their benefits are to be made clear to top management. He also recognizes that few training managers have the background, skill, and time to engage in extensive evaluations, and he suggests they call on specialists, researchers, and consultants for advice and help.

Level Four: Results (The Impact of Training on the Business)

Based on the premise that "the objectives of most training programs can be stated in terms of results such as reduced turnover, reduced costs, improved efficiency, reduction in grievances, increase in quality and quantity of production, or improved morale," Kirkpatrick concludes "it would be best to evaluate training programs directly in terms of results desired."

He recognizes there are so many complicating factors that it is extremely difficult, if not impossible, to evaluate certain kinds of programs in terms of results. He recommends that training managers evaluate in terms of reaction, learning, and behavior first and then consider tangible business results. He also cautions that due to the difficulty in the separation of variables (that is, how much of the improvement is due to training as compared to other factors), it is very difficult to measure results that can be attributed directly to a specific training program.

From Kirkpatrick's experience with level four evaluations, he concludes that it is probably better to use the personal interview rather than a questionnaire to measure results. Also, measures on a *before* and *after* basis can provide evidence (but not necessarily proof) that the business results are directly attributed to the training even though other factors might have been influential.

Chapter 7.2 includes an example of training evaluation applied to an internal CAPA program certification.

4.5 MANAGEMENT OF THE INVESTIGATION AND CAPA SYSTEM

Management of the investigation and CAPA system is perhaps the most compelling task regulated companies face today. The requirement is simple: implementing an efficient investigation and CAPA system as part of an overall QMS. Lack of compliance with the different CAPA system elements is the top observation from worldwide regulatory inspections. Weakness of the CAPA system is a true indicator of the overall regulatory and quality health of the organization. Daniel and Kimmelman[4] cited three causes for this weakness:

- Overloading of the CAPA processes
- Inadequate resources applied to the processes
- Inadequate follow-up of corrective actions

I agree with these reasons and may add a fourth: the over-customization of CAPA processes. It is almost impossible to understand the CAPA system and processes of any regulated company only by reading its investigation and CAPA documents. For some unknown reason, each regulated firm tries to complicate CAPA as much as possible. The unfortunate result is constant violation of its own procedures. Chapter 6 contains a discussion of the top symptoms of inadequate investigation and CAPA systems, including recommendations for fixing them.

To complete the introduction to this section, we will share with you the two imperative items needed to build an effective investigation and CAPA system: *time* and *resources*. Good CAPA processes require both of them and management is ultimately responsible for efficient quality processes, including investigation and CAPA processes.

4.5.1 Investigation and CAPA System Structure

Most companies do not have a formal structure devoted to investigation and CAPA processes, and almost anyone can perform investigations and CAPAs. In most companies, someone from within the quality

[4] Daniel. And Kimmelman (2008).

department acts as a reviewer of the investigation, leading to the back and forth of investigation reports. Reporting to management is usually in the form of metrics regarding how many reports are past due.

Best practices for the investigation and CAPA systems include the following:

- Dedication of full-time investigators, most often organized in cross-functional teams
- Creation of multi-departmental boards to evaluate investigations, CAPA plans, and effectiveness verifications
- Creation of an investigation and CAPA management function in charge of creating and monitoring meaningful metrics and activities

All of these are key improvement factors along with establishing risk management tools to develop and maintain an efficient investigation and CAPA system.

4.5.2 Investigation and CAPA Process Metrics and U.S. FDA's Quality Metrics program

Trending is an important tool for reporting and controlling quality processes. It is also a main requirement of the quality management system. If you do not measure your processes, you cannot manage or improve them. The only metrics most regulated firms use are those related to timeliness, and most of them are useless metrics because time requirements are rarely risk-based. A company will establish, for example, a 30-day period to complete investigations, regardless of any priority criterion. This is one of the diseases affecting our investigation and CAPA systems; Chapter 6 discusses this topic.

Regulators' expectation is that investigation and CAPA processes be completed in a reasonable time frame, commensurate with the risk and the magnitude of the event. Normally four time frames can be established and monitored:

a. Detection of the problem and initiation of the nonconformance investigation

b. Completion of the root cause investigation, including documentation and approval of the report

c. Preparation of the CAPA plan

d. Evaluation of the effectiveness of the implemented corrective or preventive actions

Firms must define adverse trends for each quality metric. When an adverse trend is identified, an investigation should be initiated to identify the root causes. From the point of view of continuous improvement and the health of the quality system, the most important information is obtained from the analysis of root causes and the evaluation of the effectiveness of corrective and preventive actions. In the first case, a simple Pareto chart can help to monitor the prevalent root causes.

Other useful metrics can be:

- Number of investigations opened during one-month period
- Number of investigations overdue during one-month period
- Number of investigations closed during one-month period
- Cycle time of investigations closed during one-month period

U.S. FDA Quality Metric Program

The FDA has identified 10 quality data points that finished dosage form and active pharmaceutical ingredient makers will need to collect to calculate four quality metrics for each product they manufacture. A draft guidance was published July 2015 on this topic.[5] Companies will need to monitor quality data on:

1. The number of lots attempted of the product;
2. The number of specification-related rejected lots of the product, whether rejected during or after manufacturing;
3. The number of attempted lots pending disposition for more than 30 days;
4. The number of out-of-specification results for the product, including stability testing;
5. The number of lot release and stability tests conducted for the product;
6. The number of OOS results for lot release and stability tests for the product that are invalidated because of a lab error;
7. The number of quality complaints received for the product;
8. The number of lots attempted that are released for distribution or for next stage of manufacturing;
9. Whether the associated annual product review or product quality review was completed within 30 days of their annual due date; and
10. The number of annual product reviews (APRs) or product quality reviews (PQRs) required for the product.

[5] http://www.fda.gov/downloads/drugs/guidancecomplianceregulatoryinformation/guidances/ucm455957.pdf

Basically, half of these data points are related to investigations and CAPA processes: items #2, #3, #4, #6, and #7.

These data will be plugged into formulas that will calculate the following four quality metrics:

1. Lot acceptance rate
2. Product quality complaint rate
3. Invalidated out-of-specification rate
4. Annual product review on time rate

Again, half of the four basic quality metrics are directly related to the investigation and CAPA system. In the proposed guidance, FDA established that any firm involved in the manufacture, preparation, propagation, compounding or processing of a finished dosage product or API must submit quality metrics data. The firm's quality control unit will be tasked with compiling the reports. The FDA assumes that drug companies will already have access to the data needed to submit such a report.

Metrics data will need to be submitted for a one-year period that will start after the FDA begins collecting the data, which has not been announced at the time of this publication. Reports must be submitted within 60 days of the end date of the reporting period, and data should be segregated in the report on a quarterly basis. Once collected, the data will be used to develop a risk-based inspection schedule, predict drug shortages, and increase the efficiency and effectiveness of inspections. Regulated companies can expect quality data to be verified during on-site inspections. If inconsistencies are found, the report's integrity may be questioned and used as an additional factor in risk-based or for-cause inspection scheduling. In addition, failure to report quality data may lead to an earlier inspection, or cause products made at the site to be deemed adulterated and subject to enforcement action.

FDA also plans to use the metrics data (along with internal FDA data such as inspection results, recalls, field alert reports, and biological product deviation reports) to identify quality problems that require correction or could result in a shortage, according to the draft. FDA is also seeking input on whether it should allow drug makers the opportunity to submit data on three optional metrics:

1. Senior management engagement
2. CAPA effectiveness
3. Process capability / performance as evidence of manufacturing robustness and a commitment to quality.

Under the draft guidance, senior management engagement and CAPA effectiveness metrics would determine "quality culture." Management engagement is used to determine if APRs or PQRs are reviewed and approved by either the head of the quality unit, the head of the operations unit, both of them or neither. CAPA effectiveness asks what percentage of a company's corrective actions involved retraining of personnel to determine if the root cause of a deviation is lack of proper training.

Process capability and performance covers three yes/no questions: whether management calculated a process capability or performance index for each critical quality attribute as part of a product's APR or PQR; whether management requires a CAPA at some lower process capability or performance index; and if so, the capability or index that triggers a CAPA.

4.5.3 Risk Management and the Investigation and CAPA System

Most of the discussion of this topic was included at the beginning of Chapter 4. Following are a few critical points we must remember:

- Always link your investigation and CAPA processes to the risk (importance and magnitude) of the event
- Provide enough resources to investigate, review, and manage your CAPA system
- Provide enough time to perform investigation and CAPA activities
- Professionalize your investigation and CAPA functions (use full-time investigators)
- Establish multi-functional boards for investigation reports evaluation and for CAPA plan activities
- Always consider your investigation and CAPA among your most critical processes

4.5.3.1 CAPA System and FMEA

In Chapter 4.1.2, we established that a preliminary evaluation of the impact of the event based on the initial data and evidence available is one of the first actions to be taken once a problem is detected. The outcome of that initial impact assessment is a determination of the level of risk. This determination will help us guide the efforts of our investigation process.

At this point, most people lose sight of a tool that has been out there for many decades to help us analyze risk and determine the actions needed to address the risk. That tool is known as failure modes and effects analysis (FMEA). It is a systematic method to identify and prevent product and process problems before they occur. Used proactively, the

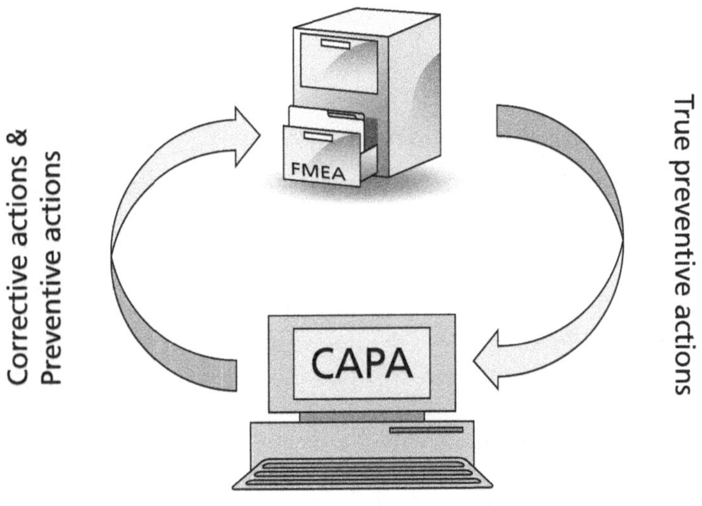

Figure 4.12 Interaction between FMEA and CAPA.

FMEA is an excellent tool of true preventive actions; those actions that can be implemented prior to the first occurrence of the failure.

Most companies do not see the direct link between the FMEA and the CAPA system. The main reason for these seems to be the fact that most of the FMEAs are developed by the technical groups, process engineers, and so on. Meanwhile, the CAPA system is mostly led by the quality group. If these teams work as silos, they will never interact in the way they are supposed to interact. Figure 4.12 shows the interaction of the FMEA and CAPA.

As can be noticed from Figure 4.12, a proactive FMEA can feed the CAPA system with true preventive actions; that is, actions that can be implemented prior to the first occurrence of the failure. On the other hand, the CAPA system provides corrective and preventive actions. As can be noticed, both systems provide for a closed-loop process. In many regulated companies the loop is not closed. For example, in many cases, the only interaction between the FMEA and CAPA start with a nonconformance. At that moment, the typical question is: "Was that failure mode included in the FMEA?" Unfortunately, the most common answer to this question is "No." The typical action is to revise the FMEA in order to include that failure mode. However, such action is reactive rather than proactive. It is like the vicious cycle we mentioned in Figure 4.3, but this time it is applied to the FMEA instead of the investigation process.

In an effective CAPA system, the answer to the question: "Was this failure mode included in the FMEA?" must be "Yes." Then, the next question should be: "Based on the FMEA, which kind of risk level does that failure mode represent: low, medium, or high?" Finally, this could be used as the basis for the risk prioritization of investigations presented previously in Figure 4.5.

4.5.4 Management of External CAPA

When the nonconformance relates to suppliers, there are differences with respect to the internal investigation and CAPA system. Perhaps the main difference is that the time frame for completing the investigation and implementing corrective or preventive action is out of our control. Most first-tier suppliers to the regulated industry have a poor quality system and very low understanding of the investigation and CAPA system.

In most cases, regulated companies will document the detected nonconforming situation, including corrections such as quarantine of the nonconforming material, and then request a full investigation and CAPA from the vendor. Contact with the vendor is established through the supplier quality group, which is responsible for getting acceptable CAPA documentation from the vendor in order to close the CAPA event. It is not recommended to apply the same time frame used for the internal investigation reports (for example, 20 or 30 days) to those vendor investigations because you will have no control over it.

Best practices for external investigation and CAPA include:

- "Educate" your supplier base about the importance of the investigation and CAPA system, and the need for timely responses to nonconformance investigations and CAPA issues.
- Include explicit investigation and CAPA responsibilities and responsiveness within the contract or quality agreement your company must establish with each of your suppliers.
- Tie the timeline for supplier response to risk and the magnitude of the nonconformance.
- Establish responsiveness metrics to measure and evaluate each supplier.
- Be ready to help suppliers with resources if your external investigation and CAPA becomes stagnant.
- Give top priority to the investigation and CAPA system during audits.

5

Human Error Investigation and Reduction

5.1 ABOUT HUMAN ERROR

For many years we considered human errors or mistakes the cause of a mishap or problem. Human error, under whatever label (procedures not followed, lack of attention, or simply error), was the conclusion of the investigation. Very often it was coupled with some kind of training activity (most frequently re-training) as corrective action. We even have an old adage—*To err is human*—to explain it. Human errors cannot be eliminated nor even significantly reduced simply by telling operators to be more careful. This simplistic approach does not work because we are not addressing any root cause. *Human error is more a symptom than a cause.*

The aim of this chapter is to focus on the human side of the quality and manufacturing errors. For the reader interested on how human errors and mistakes create accidents and huge disasters, there are numerous (and very good) authoritative sources, some of them are included in the bibliographic section of this book. It is not the intent of this chapter to discuss the numerous definitions, classifications, and approaches that have been published regarding human errors and human factors.

The way we look at the human side of the problem has evolved during the past few decades. Industrial psychologists and human reliability professionals took command during the investigation of catastrophic accidents (Chernobyl, Challenger, and aviation accidents) and these old conceptions changed. Now, we see human errors as the symptoms of deeper causes. In other words, human errors are consequences, not causes.

Most of the time, even though accidents are classified as mechanical or other kinds of failure, the roots go back to a human who made an error. For this discussion, human error excludes deliberate actions with harmful intent; these are considered sabotage. In the medical products regulated environment, the combination of human error and retraining is still indicated in the root cause and corrective action sections of many investigation reports. At this time of the twenty-first century, we can say that companies are abusing human error as a simplistic explanation for faulty quality systems. This is not a book on human reliability, but any professional working with investigations and CAPA systems must become familiar with these concepts. It is essential that we stop using human error (or any of its variations) as a root cause of our quality problems. As mentioned before, we must ask why the human made the mistake.

Human errors are not a uniform collection of unwanted acts. Lack of attention plays a significant role in all categories of human error. Slips, lapses, and mistakes are all more common when situational factors (fatigue, workload, multitasking, and boredom) divert our attention. In the regulated industries, these factors should be negligible; we should not be relying on memory for procedures and instructions. Batch records and device history records exist for that exact purpose. We must read the instructions, execute the task, and then document the action performed.

FDA and foreign regulators require the consideration of human factors during the development of medical devices. In the landmark 1996 guidance *Do It By Design—An Introduction to Human Factors in Medical Devices*, the FDA established design requirements to avoid the user errors. More recently the Agency introduced those concepts of human reliability to drug and biotechnology manufacturers.

I highly recommend that interested professionals study some of the references included on this topic. Although the oldest ones refer to aviation, nuclear, and industrial accidents, several recent books cover the hospital and healthcare industry, where human errors cost tens of thousands of lives every year in the United States alone.

To finish with the introduction to this critical area (by frequency and by significance), we must differentiate between errors (mistakes) and defects (also known as nonconformances). Regulated companies do not recall products because there were human errors during the manufacturing process. They recall products because their quality system was unable to detect the human error and the nonconformance product was distributed, becoming an adulterated and/or misbranded item.

Some statistics related to human error

- 99% of accidental losses (except for natural disasters) begin with a human error
- Root causes of the vast majority of accidents are management system weaknesses
- 8% of men are color blind while only 1/200 women have the condition
- 80% of medical product recalls due to incorrect expiration date or incorrect lot/batch number are caused by a transposition of digits

- 1.5 million Americans are injured every year by drug errors in hospitals, nursing homes, and doctor's offices (patients' own medication mix-ups are not included)
- On average, every hospitalized patient is subject to (at least) one medication error per day
- Seventeen (17) hours of work without a break is the same as being legally drunk
- Worst period for human errors: 2 am to 5 am
- About 15% of human errors are due to acquired habits
- Human error accounts for 90% of road accidents
- The rate of error and mistakes for most procedure-based tasks is 1/100
- Average workers are interrupted every 11 minutes and then spend almost 1/3 of their day recovering from these distractions

5.1.1. Data Integrity and Human Error

The integrity of data generated by a regulated company, from incoming to distribution data, with special emphasis on production and laboratory data, can make or break a regulatory inspection. It requires only a single adverse non-compliance situation to cast a shadow over all the work undertaken by a regulated company. Although some recent serious cases of data integrity breaches seem to be fraud, human errors related to documentation of production and laboratory activities can also receive this interpretation from regulatory agencies. Sloppy documentation practices (frequent date and signature omissions later fixed by back dating) are usually labeled as human error. In the past, regulatory agencies called this "careless work" but today they are frequently cited as lack of data integrity. Data integrity has five main characteristics:

1. **Attributable**—data are identified with a specific subject and a specific observer and recorder
2. **Legible**—data are readable and understandable by humans
3. **Contemporaneous**—data are recorded at the time they are generated or observed.
4. **Original**—data are recorded for the first time
5. **Accurate**—data are correct

5.2 HUMAN ERROR AND HUMAN FACTOR

Very often we use the term *human error* to implicate the human (operator, quality control analyst, inspector, and so on) as the cause of an accident or production/laboratory error. However, human error rarely refers to a single incorrect action by an operator or laboratory technician. Although individuals make errors and mistakes, it is usually because human factors issues were not properly addressed. *Human error* can be defined as a departure from acceptable or desirable practices on the part of an individual resulting in unacceptable or undesirable result.

Human factors are defined as the discipline concerned with designing machines, operations, and work environments to match human capabilities, limitations, and needs. Human factors can be further defined as any factor that influences behavior at work in a way that can negatively affect the output of the process the human is involved with. This is pretty much the concept of standard work used for decades at Toyota.

When an operator does not properly execute a manufacturing step, we immediately label it as human error. When we investigate the situation, inadequate training and supervision, and lack of clarity in the working instruction can be factors behind the operator's mistake. As you can see, this is the same scheme we have been describing since the beginning of this chapter. Human errors and mistakes are the symptoms of causal (human) factors associated with root causes that we must discover prior to solving them.

This topic of human factors falls within the field of human reliability engineering. It deals with the person-process interface and how this interaction influences the performance of people. Some authors refer to human factors as performance shaping factors (PSFs).

Human failures can be divided into two broad categories, errors and violations:

- A human *error* is an action or decision that was not intended, that involved a deviation from an accepted standard, and that led to an undesirable outcome.

  A laboratory technician performing two tests simultaneously uses the wrong sample for one of the tests.

- A *violation* is a deliberate deviation from a rule or procedure.

  A production operator fills out a cleaning record without performing the task.

Based on our experience, violations are rare within the medical product regulated industry and the vast majority of human failure can be attributed to unintended errors. Figure 5.1 depicts a classification of human errors.

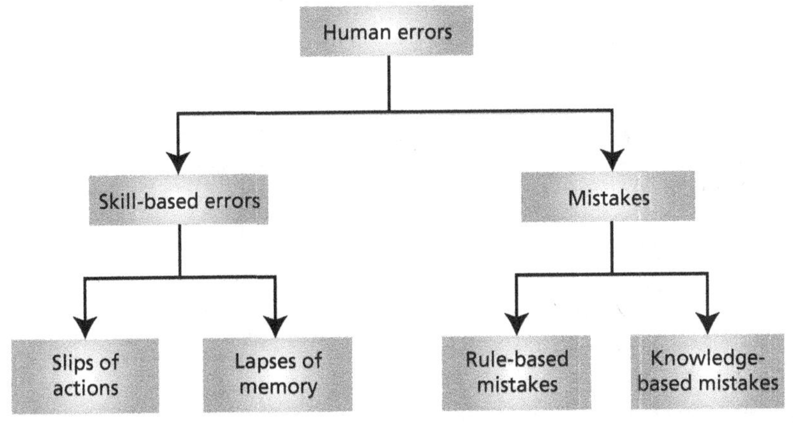

Figure 5.1 Types of human errors.

5.3 PSYCHOLOGY AND CLASSIFICATION OF THE HUMAN ERROR

Errors are a predictable consequence of basic and normally useful cognitive mechanism, not random or arbitrary processes. As error expert James Reason suggests, "Correct performance and systematic errors are two sides of the same coin."

Human errors are not a uniform collection of unwanted acts. Psychologists distinguish between *skill-based* slips and lapses, *rule-based* mistakes, and *knowledge-based* mistakes. *Skills* are highly practiced behaviors that we perform routinely with little conscious effort. They are literally automatic. Rule- and knowledge-based performance requires more mental involvement and conscious deliberation.

Slips and lapses occur in familiar tasks we can perform without much need for conscious attention (see Table 5.1). They are errors in the performance of skill-based behaviors, typically when our attention or memory is diverted and we fail to closely monitor the actions we are performing.

Slips (commission errors) are failures in carrying out the actions of a task. They can be described as "actions not as planned." Slips are errors in which the intention is correct but failure occurs when carrying out the activity required.

> *A production operator documents the wrong date in a production document.*

Table 5.1 Slips and lapses of memory.

Slips (commission or execution errors)	Lapses (omission errors)
• Operating the wrong switch control or valve • Misordering a sequence of steps • Transposing digits when printing a lot number or expiration date • Product mix-ups (incorrect label, incorrect product, both incorrect) • Failure to detect incorrect expiration date, incorrect lot number, incorrect size, or other defect during an inspection	• Equipment identification not recorded in the batch record • Omission of information that must be recorded • Omitting a step or series of steps from a task

Lapses (omission errors) cause humans to forget to carry out an action. They are defined as an error in operator recall and can be reduced by minimizing distractions and interruptions and by providing effective reminders, especially for tasks that take some time to complete or involve periods of waiting.

> *A production operator forgets to document the date in a production document.*

Mistakes are errors in rule- or knowledge-based performance. They are a more complex type of human error where we do the wrong thing believing it to be right. Mistakes include errors in perception, judgment, inference, and interpretation. Two types of mistakes exist, rule-based and knowledge-based.

Rule-based mistakes occur when our behavior is based on remembered rules or familiar procedures. We have a strong tendency to use familiar rules or solutions even when these are not the most convenient or efficient.

Knowledge-based mistakes result from misdiagnosis and miscalculation. Planning or problem solving requires that we reason from previous knowledge or use analogies.

Attention plays a significant role in all categories of human errors. Slips, lapses, and mistakes are all more common when situational factors such as fatigue, sleep loss, alcohol, drugs, illness, workload, stress, work pressure, multitasking, boredom, frustration, fear, anxiety, and anger play a role.

Violations can be defined as deliberate deviations from rules, procedures, instructions and regulations. Sometimes, violations are called intentional errors. The breaching or violating of health and safety rules or procedures is a significant cause of many accidents and injuries at work, but I don't believe that we have frequent purposeful violations of the quality system in this industry. Many companies have the documentation mechanism of planned deviations to cover such circumstances. Violations are divided into three categories: routine, situational, and exceptional.

> *A production operator documents a cleaning work that was not performed.*

We can identify a fourth class of violations: necessary. This type of violation involves situations where non-compliance is necessary to complete the job.

> *A filling operator is forced to transcribe data (a violation to contemporaneous rule of data integrity) because there is no computer terminal in the weigh monitoring station.*

In addition to this classification, there are many other ways to categorize human error.

Almost every author involved in this field has developed his own list. Several of them are so complex as to require a graduate degree in human psycho-physiology to be understood. Many of us prefer simple things, so we will discuss just two of the most frequently used classifications.

Swain and Guttman (1983) divide human error into four main groups:

- Errors of *omission* (forgetting to do something)
- Errors of *commission* (doing the task incorrectly)
- *Sequence* errors (doing something out of order)
- *Timing* errors (doing the task too slow, too fast, or too late)

Reason (1990) divides between active and latent failures. *Active* failures have an immediate consequence and are usually made by front-line workers such as drivers, control room staff, or machine operators. In a situation where there is no room for error, active failures have an immediate impact on quality or health and safety.

Latent failures are made by people whose tasks are removed in time and space from operational activities (designers, decision makers, and managers). Latent failures are typically failures in management systems (design, implementation, or monitoring). Examples of human factors behind latent failures are:

- Poor design of plant and equipment
- Inadequate procedures and work instructions
- Ineffective training
- Inadequate supervision
- Inadequate staff and resources
- Ineffective communications
- Uncertainties in roles and responsibilities

In our regulated environment, most active failures trace back to some pre-condition (latent failure). We need a good tracking and trending analysis system to be able to discover what in many cases is a true cause-and-effect relationship. One of my favorite examples can clarify this point: A medical device manufacturer has a production room with two dozen identical machines producing the same kind of subassembly product. They work 24/7 and each work station is attended by only one operator who also verifies the quality of his or her job prior to sending the pieces to the storage room. The next operation suffers from frequent defective subassembly products sent from the production room and this situation was jeopardizing the productivity of the whole plant. For a couple of years, the level of defective subassembly has been between 2 percent and 3 percent, and the impact on scrap, productivity, and rework time is in the millions of dollars.

Nonconformance investigations always pointed to inadvertent human errors (they even created a form to document the human error in the area) corrected with retraining, awareness, and occasional termination. Nothing seemed to work and the rate of error remained steady. A simple analysis (data segmentation) revealed the real situation: more than 80 percent of the bad units were produced by two work stations independent of operator, shift, or day of the week. This concentration chart of defects also revealed that these two stations were the ones situated next to the two doors of the manufacturing room. They were all-glass doors opening to the main corridor of the plant. The consequence of this location was that both corner work stations received many social visits from co-workers and obviously this represented an enormous source of distraction for operators attending these two machines.

As you can see, the latent factor creating those human errors was the layout of the facility. A simple substitution of the all-glass doors with metal doors effectively reduced the rate of defective products by more than two-thirds in just the first month. From this moment on, the defect rates for these two stations were not statistically different from the other 22 stations in the same room.

Reason[1] proposed what is known to as the "Swiss cheese model" of system failure. Every step in a process has the potential for failure. The system is analogous to a stack of Swiss cheese slices. Each hole is an opportunity for a process to fail, and each of the slices is a "defensive layer" in the process against potential error impacting the results. An error may allow a problem to pass through a hole in one layer, but in the next layer the holes are in different places; the problem should be caught. For a catastrophic error to occur (a plane crash or the distribution of a pharmaceutical product with incorrect label information), the holes must align for each step in the process. This allows all defenses to be defeated and results in an error. If the layers are set up with all the holes aligned, it becomes an inherently flawed system that will allow an error to become a final product defect. Each slice of cheese is an opportunity to stop an error. The more defenses we put up, the better. The fewer the holes and the smaller the holes, the more likely you are to notice errors that do occur.

It is important to note that the presence of holes in any one slice of our quality system may cause a final defect problem. Usually, this happens only when the holes in many slices momentarily line up to permit the result of the error to escape our controls. Reason establishes that those holes in the defenses arise for two reasons: active failures and latent pre-existing conditions, and that nearly all adverse events result from a combination of these two sets of factors.

5.4 HUMAN FACTORS

Human factors is the common term given to the widely-recognized discipline of addressing interactions in the work environment between people, the facility, and its management systems. Although individuals make errors and mistakes, it is usually because human factor issues were not properly addressed.

In addition, to be a key and critical aspect of process safety management, human factors are also the basis of a sounded process quality management. Human factors play an important role in process performance by using scientific knowledge and principles from many disciplines to reduce the frequency of errors and accidents. However, the value and importance of human factors has not yet been comprehensively accepted through the regulated industry.

A basic model for human factors relative to the process industries is shown in Figure 5.2.[2] This model identifies three main domains for human factors: Facilities and Equipment, People, and Management Systems.

[1] Reason, J. (2000).
[2] Center for Chemical Process Safety (2007).

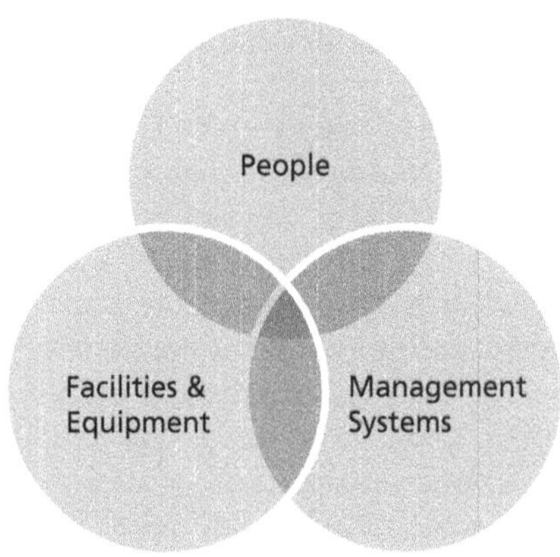

Figure 5.2 Human factor domains.

5.4.1 Compliance and Quality Culture

The importance of the compliance and quality culture in the prevention and mitigation of human failures (errors, mistakes, and violations) cannot be ignored. If we analyze how organizations are dealing with safety culture to prevent accidents, we can have a great benchmark. The inquiries into major accidents found faults in the organizational structures and procedures. These were judged to be as important as the technical and individual human failures. There is now an emphasis on the need for organizations to improve their safety culture. We can perfectly translate the following statements regarding safety culture (to prevent accidents) to our quality and compliance environment when trying to prevent errors and mistakes:

> Safety Culture—The effectiveness of self-reporting and behavioral observation programs depends greatly upon the safety culture at a site.
>
> For example: If self-reporting of impairment or reporting an impairment concern about another staff member even occasionally results in disciplinary action, then supervisors and workers will naturally be reluctant to report other staff members who appear to be impaired. On the other hand, if individuals who have come to work under some form of stress are treated fairly and with concern, personnel will report more frequently. If the company's culture emphasizes safety over other goals, personnel may be willing to turn down overtime and monitor their own fatigue levels, even if turning down the opportunity results in a loss of income.[3]

[3] Bridges, W. and Tew, R. (2010).

I did perform an analysis of more than 10,000 batches produced at one FDA-regulated plant. Not a single event was documented related to component(s) spilled out prior to charging the mixing tanks. However, more than 40 batches failed laboratory analysis due to concentration of one or more of its components below specifications. Definitively many (if not most) of these failures could be avoided if the operator(s) had notified about the spill and requested more component. Instead, fear of retaliation and punishment led to hiding those situations. Needless to say that each of those 40 failure investigations was a nightmare; laboratory results showed lack of adequate quantity of components while pristine production batch documentation showed that everything was perfect!

For many companies the use of electronic records can have unexpected benefits— exposing cheaters. A few examples can illustrate this:

> Five components (raw materials) must be added in a pre-established order (as stated in the batch record) to a mixer to produce a batch. The review of the electronic batch data revealed that all components (near 759 kg) were added within a mere 26 seconds period, which is nearly impossible. The fact is that instead of adding each component and recording its addition to the bulk, manufacturing operators added all the five components and then proceeded to document those additions. This is a violation of the batch records and the regulatory requirements.
>
> Another example relates to the documentation of activities: a cleaning equipment documentation form was printed at 16:23:37 (as per its footer printed information). However, this form was used to document activities performed several hours before, which is a violation of the contemporaneous and direct data recording attributes (see Chapter 5.1.1 for more details about data integrity).
>
> A third example also exposed lack of accuracy of recorded data: the electronic batch record requires documenting the start and the stop of a mixing step required to last at least five minutes. Start of mixing was recorded in the electronic document as 14:03 and the stop of mixing as 14:08. When the electronic record was audited it was discovered that the real time when the stop of mixing was recorded was 14:05:22. Another cheater caught!

Every group of people develops a "culture"—shared attitudes, beliefs and ways of behaving. In an organization with a good compliance and quality culture, everyone puts those elements high on the list. Everyone shares accurate perceptions of the risks to compliance and quality, and adopts the same positive attitudes to compliance and quality. This influences the ways in which individuals in the group handle new events and decisions.

Some key aspects of an effective quality and compliance culture include:

- Positive, blame-free environment towards errors and mistakes
- Good ways of informing and consulting the workforce
- Recognition of the fact that everyone has a role to play
- Commitment by top management to involving the workforce
- Cooperation between employees
- Open two-way communications
- High quality of training

The compliance and quality culture of an organization is an important factor in controlling human failures. Key factors for a positive culture include among others: open communications, management commitment and leadership, and the availability of resources.

5.4.2 Workplace Involvement: Motivation and Attention

Attention and motivation are often identified as causes for error. "Inattention to detail" is frequently cited as root cause or causal factor in human error investigation. The evidence supporting this conclusion is often weak and determining the role of lack or attention or motivation in a human error is very difficult.

Attention and motivation are internal states that cannot be measured directly. During an investigation, real-time, objective measures of attention or motivation cannot be obtained because the investigation necessarily occurs after the fact. As a result, the investigator must rely on self-reports and inference, which are subject to bias and inaccuracies.

Attributing accident and quality incidents to workers' lack of attention, attitudes, or motivations is a common practice. In the absence of compelling evidence that some characteristic of the work environment affected the workers' actions, investigators may resort to the "default" explanation and conclude that the workers were not paying attention or lacked the motivation to perform their work correctly. We never asked the next why: Why did the operator lack attention?

Many company programs, policies, and practices are intended to reduce errors associated with attention and motivation. Some programs directly focus on these potential causes and contributors to error, such as human factors engineering programs. Others may indirectly affect attention and motivation during task performance. Company elements or programs that may be implicated in errors caused by attention or motivation include:

- Poor or inadequate human factors design
- Lack of accurate and easily accessible procedures
- Performance evaluation process/human resources
- Weakness in supervision
- Weakness in problem identification and resolution programs
- Inattention to employee concerns

5.4.3 Adequate Supervision and Staffing

Nowadays many organizations are structured so as to have insufficient supervision of jobs. Supervision can and normally does play a key role in the selection of the right worker for the job, scheduling of workers to match the required tasks for the day/week, and generally overseeing the task execution to ensure policies and procedures are followed. Supervisors are not always trained on all of their key roles in support of control of human factors, such as detecting issues in workers related to fitness for duty or fatigue.

An adequately staffed organization ensures that personnel are available with the proper qualifications for both planned and foreseeable unplanned activities. Staffing is a dynamic process in which plant management monitors personnel performance to ensure that overall organizational performance goals are met or exceeded. The result of an effective staffing process is a balance between personnel costs and the achievement of organizational goals. Issues with staffing may include:

- Selection of right staff for a job
- Avoiding staff overload
- Rotating staff for tasks that require high concentration

Each organization requires the proper amount and type of expertise to competently operate under a variety of conditions. The term *expertise* includes the attributes of talent, effectiveness, knowledge, skills, abilities, and experience necessary to operate and maintain plant systems, structures, and components.

Fatigue and shift work

Many individuals work shift systems, work at night, or work very extended hours. Such working patterns can lead to adverse effects upon health, particularly for night workers. Reduced levels of performance have been associated with night work, which can also increase the likelihood of human errors. Some people experience severe fatigue at work. This can lead to poorer performance on tasks that require attention, decision-making, or high levels of skill. Too often, fatigue (as happens with multitasking) is seen as a familiar and acceptable part of everyday life. Working long hours may even be accepted in the culture of a workplace as "the thing to do."

Shift scheduling may also affect the likelihood that personnel will show performance decrements due to fatigue. Job performance may be poorer on shift work especially when working night shifts. Tasks tend to be completed more slowly at night, although this can be balanced by altering the workload. In general, the early hours of the morning (between 02:00 and 05:00) present the highest risk for fatigue-related incidents. Sleep loss can lead to lowered levels of alertness. Cumulative sleep loss over a number of days can result in a "sleep debt" with much reduced levels of productivity and attention. Such sleep loss results not only from working night shifts, but also on morning shifts with very early start times and from "on call" situations where it may be difficult to plan when to sleep. A change in the assigned shift or a rotating shift schedule will disrupt circadian rhythms and may increase the likelihood of errors. Although companies establish limits for work hours to reduce on-the-job fatigue, there is a lot of room for improvement. It has been shown that 17 hours of work without a break is the same as being legally drunk.

5.4.4 Procedures and Task Design

Many of the procedures, working instructions, and reference documents do not follow best practices for controlling human error, and so the written process actually contributes to increased error rates. Many organizations have lengthy procedures, that are poorly written and disorganized. Deficient procedures are one of the most prevalent problems in process industries since procedures have not traditionally been developed from the perspective of optimizing human factors; instead, procedures have been traditionally developed to meet a compliance requirement to have written procedures. For procedures to be effective, they must be used. Organizations must also address the reasons that cause workers not to use the written procedure. Examples of procedure inaccuracies that prevent their use include:

- Procedures are difficult to use in the work environment
- Procedures are difficult to understand
- Procedures are incorrect or incomplete (users need more information than the procedures contain)
- Procedures has a poor format

Writing better procedures

Written procedures have a critical role in maintaining consistency and in ensuring that everyone has the same basic level of information and instructions. They are a key element of the quality management system and an important training tool. However, poor procedures can be a reason for people to not follow required actions. In addition to being technically accurate, procedures need to be well-written, usable and up to date. Ask yourself:

- Are your procedures accessible?
- Are they actually followed by staff?
- Are they written so that they can be understood and followed easily?
- Do they reflect the tasks as they are actually carried out?
- Do they include all required information and/or instructions?
- Are they current and reviewed periodically?

Procedures must:

- Be accurate and complete
- Be clear and concise with an appropriate level of detail
- Be accessible, current, and up-to-date
- Be supported by training
- Use adequate and comprehensible language
- Use consistent terminology
- Reflect how tasks are actually carried out
- Promote ownership by users

Start by collecting information about the task and the users. To do this you could carry out an activity analysis. Here are some issues to think about:

- Consider both the difficulty and importance of the task to be documented
- Find out how often the task is carried out
- Think about who will use the procedure and the level of information they will need
- Establish the skills, experience level, past training, and needs of the users of the procedure

- Look the level of training needed to support the understanding and effective use of the procedure
- Try to involve users in the preparation and maintenance of the procedure

Procedures can appear in different forms, for example as printed text documents, or electronically, or as quick job aids. It is important that users know where the procedures can be found and that this location is convenient for them. If it takes too long to find a procedure, users will be more reluctant to use it.

Writing style is a very important factor. As general guideline, keep sentences short and avoid complex sentence structure. This will make the procedure easier to read and understand. Try to write the required actions that users need to do in positive active sentences. For example, "Add component A and then mix for ten minutes." This is easier to follow than the more complicated "After adding component A, then start to mix" or "Do not mix until component A has been added." Write actions in the order in which they need to be carried out.

Divide longer procedures into shorter pieces. This helps users to go back to a particular step if they are interrupted or if the task takes some time to carry out. AVOID USING ALL CAPITAL LETTERS FOR THE TEXT. Research shows that this is slower and more difficult to read than lower case text. Decide how features such as capitals, bold, italics, and underlining will be used. Overuse of these features is very distracting for users.

Avoid using very small fonts (for example, 8 point or smaller) as this is very difficult for users to read.

Make good use of open space in the printed text. Cluttered pages are more difficult to read. Although the procedure may have more pages, providing spaces between steps on the page will make it more usable. Try to use the same format and structure for all procedures. An inconsistent format could confuse the user.

Task Design

A task that is designed with the human limits in mind is much more likely to work effectively than one that assumes humans can and will "always" do what is written. The task must consider that humans think and remember and factor in prior data and prior experiences. Take into consideration the complexity of each task. If the task is too complex, then humans can forget their place in the task, fail to understand the goal of each step or sub-step, or fail to notice when something isn't going right. Task complexity is a function of many factors, among them:

- Number of choices available for making a wrong selection of similar items (such as number of similar switches, number of similar valves, number of similar size and shaped cans)
- Number of parallel tasks that may distract the worker from the task at hand (leading to either an initiating event or failure of a protection layer)
- Number of staff involved (more staff = more complex)
- Number of adjustments or steps necessary to achieve the goal
- Amount of mental math required (as a rule, no math in anyone's head should be required when accomplishing a standardized task)
- The amount of judgment required to know when the goal has been accomplished within the task
- The amount of feedback in the process required to allow the operator or lab technician to realize (in time) that they made a mistake
- Where the task is to be performed: too noisy, too cold, too hot, too distracting, too dark?

Activity analysis

It is often helpful to look at a particular job, task or activity in a given work setting. One approach is to understand what the job actually consists of and what risks are involved. This is known as task or activity analysis. To try it, select a particular activity or task and find the answers to the questions below:

1. Who does this activity?
2. Exactly what tasks/action do they do?
3. What tools or equipment are needed?
4. What decisions are made?
5. What information is needed to do the task?
6. Where does this information come from (people/paper/computers/displays)?
7. How is the task learned?
8. How is competence assessed?
9. How often is the activity carried out?
10. Where is the task carried out?
11. What is the working environment like (temperature, noise, lighting and so on)?

12. Are there time constraints on the task?
13. What can go wrong?
14. Where is there potential to make errors?
15. How can failures be detected and corrected?

You will find it easier if you ask someone who does the activity to walk through it with you. The aim is to find out what *really* happens, not just what *should* happen. Working through the questions, you will identify problems that need attention and you will be able to feed the results of your analysis into a risk assessment.

Improving job design

When thinking about improving job satisfaction and reducing stress levels, organizations often focus on the individual worker through the provision of stress management courses and employee assistance programs. Throughout the years, jobs have tended to become increasingly monotonous and controlled. Many jobs are designed to minimize skill requirements, maximize management control, and minimize the time required to perform a task. Jobs designed like this have a human cost in terms of negative attitudes to the job and poor mental and physical health. Many attempts have been made to redesign such work to improve the quality of working life.

Such redesign is based on increasing one or more of the following job characteristics:

- Variety of tasks or skills (increased use of capabilities)
- Autonomy (higher control over when and how tasks are done)
- Completeness (whether a job produces an identifiable end result, which makes the task more significant and meaningful for the worker)
- Feedback from the job (improved knowledge of the results of the work activities)

Other characteristics of work that are also thought to be important for job satisfaction are the amount and quality of social interaction with co-workers, responsibility for technology and output, and the mental demands of a job including the need to pay close, constant attention to a task and the need to diagnose and solve problems.

Work redesign

Typical ways to job redesign include job rotation, and horizontal or vertical job enlargement. Employee involvement and participation of staff in job, task and equipment design and redesign is an important tool in the reduction of both stress levels and safety risks. Individuals are often able to identify and propose solutions to some of the ergonomic problems in their workplace. However, such initiatives need to have the support of management to make them work. Extended use of participation can create raised expectations for employees that may be difficult to meet. Employee involvement can appear threatening to managers who are used to making their own decisions.

Job redesign usually has a positive impact on job satisfaction, motivation, employee mental health, and performance as long as it is not restricted to just increasing job variety. Such redesign usually occurs in combination with other changes such as staffing levels, pay rates, or management style, which are likely to also affect these outcomes.

Error-proof operation design considerations

When incorporated into the design, error-proof mechanisms are very powerful in improving system reliability. These mechanisms, by design, will not allow a user to execute an incorrect operation. For example, if a user enters a value that is outside the accepted range of operation, the control logic will not accept the value.

5.4.5 Training and Performance

Training provides skills and/or knowledge to adequately perform a job. Personnel should be qualified to do the operations that are assigned to them in accordance with the nature of, and potential risk of, their operational activities. On the other hand, managers should define appropriate qualifications for each position to help ensure that individuals are assigned appropriate responsibilities. Personnel should also understand the effect of their activities on the product and the customer. Job descriptions should include requirements such as scientific and technical knowledge, process and product knowledge, and/or risk assessment abilities to appropriately execute certain functions.

Continued training is critical to ensure that the employees remain proficient in their operational functions. Typical training should cover the policies, processes, procedures, and written instructions related to operational activities, the product/service, the quality system, and the desired work culture. Training should focus on both the employees' specific job functions and the related regulatory requirements. Managers are expected to establish training programs that include the following:

- Evaluation of training needs
- Provision of training to satisfy these needs
- Evaluation of effectiveness of training
- Documentation of training and/or re-training

Finally, when operating in a robust quality system environment, it is important that managers verify that skills gained from training are implemented in day-to-day performance.

5.4.6 Examples of Human Factors in Process Operations

Human error is much more likely than equipment failure. Instead of trying to adapt the human to the facility, it is essential to design plants that meet the capabilities of the human. The design of control systems in process and manufacturing plants directly impacts the likelihood of human errors by operators. Consequently, the development of an optimized interface between the processes and equipment being controlled and the operators is vital for ensuring safety and operability to avoid adverse impacts on people, the process, or the company. There are various important aspects of the control system including equipment design, process control design, the human/computer interface, operating procedures and the documentation used, and operator competence.

People control processes by interacting with equipment. Process equipment includes displays, alarms, controls, computers, manual equipment and personal protective equipment. Human factors issues for process equipment relate to how people interact with and use equipment and the characteristics of the equipment that may increase the likelihood of human failures when people use it. This entails studying the match between the attributes of people and those of equipment that are involved in the interactions.

The human/computer interface deals with how people interact with computer systems with the objective of ensuring that computer system designs are functional, easily operable, efficient, and safe. Many plants today utilize computer systems to control processes. Human failures in interacting with control systems can result in loss of control and serious accidents and/or quality incidents.

Various human factor issues are important in developing procedures. Also, a variety of documentation is used, including manuals, guidelines, checklists, data sheets, logs, records, work orders, and so on. Documentation design can have a major impact on process safety and operability. Procedures that are not followed, guidelines that are not used, diagrams that are misleading, and records that are not completed properly can all increase the likelihood of errors.

The ability of personnel to perform tasks according to expectations, or the competence of personnel, is fundamental to every organization because of the role it plays in ensuring tasks are carried out satisfactorily.

Table 5.2[4] depicts a comparison between human and machine capabilities.

[4] Center for Chemical Process Safety (2007).

Table 5.2 Comparison between human and machine capabilities.

Humans excel in	Machines excel in
• Detection of certain forms of very low energy • Sensitivity to an extremely wide variety of stimuli • Perceiving patterns and making generalization about them • Ability to store large amounts of information for long periods—and recalling relevant facts at appropriate moments • Ability to exercise judgement where events cannot be completely defined • Improvising and adopting flexible procedures • Ability to react to unexpected low-probability events • Applying originality in solving problems (alternative solutions) • Ability to profit from experience and alter course of action • Ability to perform fine manipulations, especially where misalignment appears unexpected • Ability to continue to perform when overloaded • Ability to reason inductively	• Monitoring (both people and machines) • Performing routine, repetitive, or very precise operations • Responding very quickly to control signals • Storing and recalling large amount of information in short time periods • Performing complex and rapid computations with high accuracy • Sensitivity to stimuli beyond the range of human sensitivity (infrared, radio waves) • Doing many things at one time • Exerting large amounts of force smoothly and precisely • Insensitivity to extraneous factors • Ability to repeat operations very rapidly, continuously, and precisely the same way over a long period • Operating in environments that are hostile and beyond human tolerance • Deductive process

In the United States, FDA includes human factors as a critical element to consider during medical devices' design process. The FDA's Human Factors Pre-Market Evaluation Team ensures that new medical devices have been designed to be reasonably safe and effective when used by the intended user populations. The effort primarily involves reviewing new device submissions, promoting effective and focused human factors evaluation and good design practices for medical devices. Human factors/usability engineering focuses on the interactions between people and devices. The critical element in these interactions is the device user interface. To understand the human-machine system, it's important to understand the ways that people:

- Perceive information from the device,
- Interpret the information and make decisions about what to do, and
- Manipulate the device, its components, and/or its controls.

It's also important to understand the ways that devices:

- React to input from the user, and then
- Provide feedback to the user about the effects of their actions.

Human factors/usability engineering is used to design the machine-human (device-user) interface. The user interface includes all components with which users interact while preparing the device for use (for example, unpacking, set up, calibration), using the device, or performing maintenance (for example, cleaning, replacing a battery, making repairs). For medical devices, the most important goal of the human factors/usability engineering process is to minimize use-related hazards and risks and then confirm that these efforts were successful and users can use the device safely and effectively.

5.5 HOW ORGANIZATIONS DEAL WITH HUMAN ERRORS

An increasing number of regulated companies are establishing specific procedures to deal with this plague of human errors. Some divert the human error investigation to human resources. Others develop a checklist to search for specific human factors that could be considered precursors to the incident under investigation. The main point here is not who is in charge of the investigation, but rather what tools and knowledge they have to perform a good and effective investigation. Most regulated companies still do not "get" the human factor message and focus their investigations solely on the carelessness of their associates.

Manufacturing errors are usually costly in the medical product industry, especially when the products involved reach the customers and must be recalled. A recent case of a pill coated with the incorrect color resulted in the dismissal of the entire crew involved with the manufacture of the batch.

An FDA inspector recently discovered some backdated information. In response to the finding, the company stated that "the employees involved will be retrained and warned that a future recurrence will have zero tolerance resulting in severe action, including possible immediate termination." Several questions arise: Why did the associates backdate the information? Did management control exist to prevent or even detect this behavior? The warning letter indicates that this was a repeat observation following two previous inspections. We may conclude that many regulated companies are not dealing appropriately with human error, and some of them are not dealing with it at all.

5.6 INVESTIGATING HUMAN ERRORS

After any incident involving human failure, there may be an investigation into the causes and contributing factors. Very often, little attempt is made to understand why the human failures occurred and the tendency is to blame someone for the error. The obvious solution, most of the time, is to retrain, counsel, discipline, or dismiss that employee.

However, finding the human factors that cause those incidents is the key to preventing similar reoccurrences through the design of effective control measures. We must realize that practically all incidents attributed to human errors are symptoms of a breakdown in management systems. We must investigate "human error" as we do with any other nonconformance or deviation within our quality system. We have a symptom and we must discover its causal factors (human factors in this case) in order to identify the root cause. The main point to consider is that we are finger-pointing at some of our associates as responsible for the situation, and we must allow them to express their opinions. Interviewing the workers involved is the most important method used to investigate the "human errors." When interviewing the personnel involved in the event, we are not just asking questions, we are trying to discover why this person did not follow the procedure or why this person made a decision that later created the problem. The main objective of the investigation is to gather all relevant facts. Chapter 8.4.3 contains 50 questions that can be used as a guidance during the investigation of human errors. The purpose of these questions is to obtain a better understanding of the human factors surrounding the issue under investigation.

You Are Interviewing, Not Interrogating

The conversation formats usually identified with a quality audit or nonconformance investigation will range from informal conversation with witnesses to a tense confrontation with the person believed responsible for the questionable action. The division between the two extremes is not a clear-cut line of separation. The more distant people are from an incident, the less concerned they are about repercussions; the closer they are to the incident, the more stressed or concerned they become in talking about the situation. The concern can be due to knowledge of the action, actual involvement in the incident, or fear of being held responsible for the actions of others.

The objective of an effective interview is to gain knowledge and information that are pertinent to the investigation. The characteristics of an effective interview include the following:

- It is a non-threatening format and the tone is non-accusatory
- It takes a relatively short time to complete (15 minutes to one hour)
- It asks open-ended questions
- The conversation could be conducted with or without total privacy
- A formal written report of the conversation should follow

Prepare Yourself before Initiating the Interview

An experienced interviewer understands the correct questions to ask and grasps the answers that flow from the conversation. This particular skill is enhanced by advanced study and knowledge of the topic or process being discussed. If the investigator is ignorant of the process or the specific problem, the employee can take advantage of the lack of knowledge. The assimilation of sufficient background information will allow the interview team to quickly recognize inaccurate or inconsistent answers to pertinent questions. Knowledge and competence allow the investigator to enter the interview process with more confidence and self-assurance. Many times the person being interviewed will phrase answers based upon a perception of knowledge possessed by the investigator.

Opening the Interview

The meeting is expected to begin on a friendly, yet professional, tone with no defensiveness or hostility anticipated from either party. This sense of cooperation begins with the interviewer. Arrogance, aggressiveness, and an air of superiority interfere with an investigator's ability to solicit answers and assistance from the other party of the conversation. The interviewer should expect that some nervousness, even resentment, will be evident during an interview concerning an incident that may cost a lot of money and even result in a regulatory action such as a product recall.

This attitude generally subsides within a short time and both parties can then get on with the task of resolving a problem. An initial exchange with nonspecific, generic conversation allows time for both parties to adjust to the dynamics of the beginning the interview. The investigator should inform the interviewee of the identity of the persons conducting the interview and the general nature of the investigation. Inflammatory words such as "fraud" or "violation" should be replaced by "review," "analyze," "examine," "unusual things," and other phrases that generate less tension.

Control the Interview Process

While it is important to begin the interview on a friendly, non-threatening basis, it is just as important to maintain firm control over the interview process. The investigator is in charge and has a mission to accomplish: to resolve the topic of the investigation. The interview should be conducted in a business place with a minimum of distractions or potential interruptions. The conversation should be limited to the subject matter at hand.

The investigator can come prepared with a list of questions that will serve as a reminder of the topics to be discussed and specific points to be covered. The list should not become a barrier that inhibits a smooth flow of dialogue. Chapter 8.4.3 includes a form that can be used during the interview to help in the process of gathering facts and data.

Allow Sufficient Time to Answer the Question

Many times the inexperienced investigator will ask a question and immediately begin to provide the answers before the other person has an opportunity to speak. The goal is to listen to the response, not to articulate a response. Information is gained by asking a question and listening carefully to the response.

Silence can be a strong motivator to the flow of information. Once the question is asked, wait for the answer. Silence is an obvious clue that you are waiting for a response. Allow the person being interviewed to fill the silence with information. The more the person talks, the more information you will gain from the process. Additional conversation allows you to evaluate the completeness and accuracy of the responses and detect indicators of inconsistency.

Be Alert to Nonverbal Communication

Most people have a tendency to subconsciously react when giving intentionally fabricated answers to questions. Reactions may be subtle but easily recognized by an experienced investigator. Investigators should be alert to the following nonverbal communication clues that may be an indication of deception:

- Excessive grooming or fidgeting during the interview, especially during key questions
- Avoidance of eye contact during pertinent questions
- Preoccupation or fidgeting with other items on the desk or in the room
- Excessive nervousness, heavy breathing, or fast heartbeat

The effective investigator should not place too much reliance on any one factor, but should view the overall communication patterns displayed by the individual. A single gesture or motion should not be taken out of context, but rather viewed as a part of an individual's total reaction pattern. The skilled investigator must observe and analyze such points as eye movement, body gestures, and even posture in an effort to capture the full meaning of the verbal responses given to the questions.

Ending the Interview

Investigators should paraphrase or repeat key points that come from the dialogue. This ensures that the facts are understood and that nothing has been misinterpreted. Hostility should be avoided and an effort should be made to ensure that the interview ends on a positive note.

In closing, the investigator should mention the possibility of a re-contact. This might prompt an individual to "recall an important fact." An effective technique is to re-interview a critical witness in an effort to clarify a point; this gives the person a second chance to disclose significant information that is unknown to the investigator. Many witnesses are reluctant to discuss what they really know or strongly suspect. Asking "What do you think...?" allows the person being interviewed to respond.

Finally, it's essential to document the result of the interview as soon as possible and give a copy to the person interviewed for review.

5.7 ROOT CAUSES RELATED TO HUMAN PERFORMANCE: MY OWN FINDINGS WITHIN THE REGULATED INDUSTRY

In Chapter 5.4 we discussed several categories of root causes directly related to the human side of manufacturing and process industry problems. Three categories (personal performance, human reliability factors, and management and supervision) encompass many of the human factors we discuss in that chapter. Other categories (training, procedures, and so on) are also directly related to employee performance.

Here is a personal account based on direct observation and analysis of dozens of regulated manufacturing plants. The first interesting finding is that medical device manufacturers have a lot of benchmarking to do with drug manufacturer peers. When you walk the floor of a classic drug or biotech manufacturing facility, you see that operators have in front of them the corresponding working instructions (batch record). This interesting approach combines working instructions and manufacturing records into a single quality document.

As an example, if the working instruction requires a mix between 30 and 60 minutes, the document will allow space to record when the mix started and when it was stopped (time on/time off). This format has several advantages:

- The operator need not memorize how many minutes the mixer must be running
- Writing down those times allows the worker and auditors to double check that the requirement was meet
- If this step is judged to be critical, a second operator can verify its correctness
- Further audit of the document (by manufacturing and finally by quality assurance) will provide additional opportunities to detect any error before the product is released to the market

By contrast, when you walk the floor of most medical device manufacturers, no matter how high-tech their devices (from gloves or dental floss to highly sophisticated life-sustaining machines), you rarely see an employee reading and following a working instruction. Most of the time, the instructions are not concurrently used during manufacturing steps. An operator deprived of these critical instruments must rely on memory. When errors occur, employees typically receive a retraining along with a warning for not following procedures. Nobody asks what happened at the exact moment when the employee had the lapse that created this defect.

Improving working instruction and records is the first crucial step you must take if you want to reduce human errors and mistakes. Very few companies (I only know one case) actually have formal training for document writers. The result is the perpetuation of ill-written procedures and working instructions filled with incorrect or incomplete information. We must recover the essence of a GMP-regulated environment. The starting point must be better manufacturing instructions. Following are just a few examples of badly written instructions:

- Mix well
- Stick together for a few seconds
- Verify all parameters

The second key observation relates to the training system. It must be the second observation, because how do you effectively train someone in a procedure that is not clear? Here are some important thoughts:

- Today, most training provided to operators and technicians is merely the reading of less-than-perfect material (SOP, working instructions, and so on).
- Almost never is there real training material (such as PowerPoint presentations and flowcharts) or discussion of the material with trainees.

- Training conditions are far from ideal, taking place at the end of a work shift or conducted by less-than-adequate instructors without any pedagogical background.
- Almost nobody has a formal process to measure the effectiveness of training efforts and the only factor considered during human error investigations is the existence of a training sheet sign-off.
- If the employee has signed this piece of paper, training is immediately discounted as a causal factor for this event.

The third critical item is the lack of adequate supervision. Merriam-Webster's dictionary defines supervision as "the action, process, or occupation of supervising." It also defines it as "a critical watching and directing (as of activities or a course of action)." In today's manufacturing environment within regulated industries, it is difficult to find a supervisor who meets that definition. Supervising dozens of operators, spending hours every day in unproductive meetings, and dealing with bureaucracy (time card revision and adjustment, payroll, and so on) are just some of the reasons that explain the lack of adequate and effective supervision. We can add to this the fact that the supervisor's office is often far from his/her workers, which makes the supervisory function even more difficult.

Regarding these last two items, there is no difference between drug and devices manufacturers. Both have the same urgent opportunities related to training and effective supervision.

5.8 HUMAN ERROR AND RETRAINING

Let's talk about the use of retraining in the CAPA context. The definition of retrain is to train again. Every time I see retraining under the corrective or preventive action sections of CAPA documentation, I ask myself the same questions: "What is the difference between this (re) training and the original training? If a person did not follow a procedure, why is retraining the solution?" Perhaps it would be better to determine why the procedure was not followed.

Moreover, if retraining is the corrective action, the original training must be the root cause of the problem we are trying to fix (remember the definition of root cause). In other words, our original training was not effective. If we retrain with the same content, the same instructor, and the same conditions, why would it be effective this time?

The root cause of lapses and slips (see Chapter 5.3) is rarely associated to training. A hypothetical example can illustrate this: One operator forgot to perform a step during the manufacture of a batch. The same employee prepared dozens of batches of the same product during the previous months, the last one only three days ago. Due to the "error" he made today he receives a retraining. Does he really need a retraining? I think not.

Training or re-training is the appropriate corrective action when the human error is a knowledge-based mistake (see Chapter 5.3). Sometimes, staff retraining is misused as a preventive action for such incidents. It cannot be a preventive action because, in any case, it will avoid recurrence, which is the definition of corrective action. Discussing the situation with other employees to make them aware of the situation can be considered a preventive action because it will prevent the (first-time) occurrence of the situation (for those other employees).

During our training sessions, we use the analogy that the abuse of human error and retraining combination is killing our training system because we are assigning blame to our training system for all those human failures without objective evidences. Retraining is often substituted by refresher, awareness, counseling, orientation, and so on, but all of them pointing to the same inefficient and inadequate corrective or preventive actions.

This reliance on the human error and retraining combination is not adequate. Human errors are sharp indicators of the presence of underlying problems in the quality system that cannot (and will not) be properly solved by retraining. Therefore, our recommendation is to think twice the next time you are concluding that a person made an error when he/she did not follow a procedure and retraining he/she will avoid the reoccurrence of the same situation.

5.9 WORKING FROM MEMORY

About 80% of calls received by corporate help desks are due to a missing password.

When you walk through manufacturing or QC areas, you rarely see operators or analysts reading procedures or working from instructions. Very frequently, they work from memory, which is problematic because our memories fail very often. Memory gaps and errors are frequent and can occur due to a number of different reasons. As the retention interval between memorizing and retrieval of the memory lengthens, there is an increase in both the amount of information that is forgotten, and the likelihood of a memory error occurring.

Lack of attention and memory plays a significant role in all categories of human errors. Slips, lapses, and mistakes are all more common when situational factors divert our attention. However, in the regulated industries, these factors should be negligible because we are not supposed to rely on our memory to remember how to do things. Batch records, device master, and device history files exist for one purpose.

5.10 MULTITASKING AND HUMAN ERRORS

Multitasking leads to errors and mistakes.

As someone once said: "Multitasking is merely the opportunity to screw up more than one thing at a time." Multitasking is a contradictory concept. Almost everyone accepts it as an effective way of working, and many job descriptions include it as one of the most desirable behaviors. But the reality is that multitasking is neither effective nor efficient. There are multiple scientific papers to prove that multitasking is actually a very inefficient way to do things and it is at the core of many errors and mistakes. Multitasking means combining two or more activities, potentially causing at least one to receive inadequate attention. When you try to do two things at the same time, you will not be able to do either one well.

The multitasking concept was developed to describe computers, not people. But not even a CPU multitasks; it merely switches back and forth between tasks several thousand times per second, thus giving the illusion that everything is happening simultaneously. Today it's interpreted to mean multiple tasks being done simultaneously by a person. Let be clear, a majority of individuals can actually do two or more things at once, such as walk and chew gum, as the saying goes. Yes, we can walk and chew gum, but not much else.

The military even has an expression for it; they called it "task saturation"—trying to do too many things at one time. Humans cannot focus on two or more things at once. Unlike computers, we cannot make partitions on our brain to work on different tasks at the same time. We simply are not wired for that.

Repeatedly dropping and picking up a task results in greater mental fatigue and more error than deep immersion in a single task. When we are distracted, our brain processes and sorts information ineffectively. Multitasking negatively affects concentration.

Research estimates that workers are interrupted every 11 minutes and then spend almost a third of their work shift trying to recover from these distractions. In other words, we lose almost 30 percent of an average workday due to multitasking ineffectiveness.[5] When we switch between tasks, our brain jumps back and forth. It always takes some time to start a new task and restart the one you quit, and there's no guarantee that you will be able to pick up exactly where you left off. Task switching pays a tremendous toll in terms of slips and lapse errors.

A better term to define what we normally do is divide our attention. We can drive and maintain a phone conversation, but our attention gets divided. In many cases, if the conversation is really important, we will

[5] Keller, G. (2012)

try to find a safe place, stop the car, and focus solely on the conversation. There is no such thing as dividing attention between two conscious activities. We cannot make two conscious decisions at the same time, not matter how simple they are. Do you want your surgeon multitasking (for example, texting) while operating on you? Multitaskers make more errors than non-multitaskers.

In a 2009 series of articles, the New York Times reported on the dangers of driving while using cell phones to talk or to text. It reported that 16 percent of all traffic fatalities in U.S. and nearly half a million of injuries are caused every year by distracted driving. Several studies suggested that the most innocent and casual phone conversation while driving takes nearly 40 percent of your attention, practically having the same effect as being drunk.

Because of the lack of focused attention originated from multitasking, I included a specific question (#31 of 50) among those recommended for investigation human errors. (See Chapters 5.6 and 8.4.3 for details about investigating human errors).

5.11 HOW TO REDUCE THE PROBABILITY OF HUMAN ERROR

Once we all agree that eliminating all human error is impossible (to do that, we would first have to eliminate all humans), our efforts should address two areas:

- Reducing the probability of human error from the onset, and when the unavoidable error occurs,
- Implementing barriers to detect those human errors and/or to minimize their impact on the quality of our processes.

Using the CAPA concepts, these mitigation efforts have two parts:

- The preventive part must encompass important human factors such as better supervision, better procedures and working instructions, and more effective training efforts. Make your processes and your documents as error proof as you can. Do not hesitate to overuse mistake-proofing features also known by the Japanese term of *poka-yoke*.
- For the reactive part you must improve your investigations. Don't accept human error as the root cause; dig into the human factors and think twice before use retraining as a corrective action.

Companies often act as if workers make mistakes simply because they forget the instructions. They believe that retraining will help workers to not forget in the future. This lack of understanding of human error is one of the root causes of our lack of effectiveness when trying to fix human-caused defects. To succeed at error control and reduction, we must consider the influence the following factors have on behavior and performance:

- Design of facilities and equipment
- Information content and format (procedures, work instructions, and job aids)
- Training
- Method of work: Supervision and management controls (including adequate resources and clear roles and responsibilities)
- Process of communications

Do not operate from memory. Read, execute, and document is the best recipe to minimize most of the human error created by lapses of memory. Finally, but not less important, we must monitor the performance of the human involved in our process. Simple statistical tools such as the analysis of proportions or *chi-squared* can help. The methodic identification of the best performer (who can be used for benchmarking purposes) and of the not-so-best can help the organization to improve whole processes, from job description adequacies to the best way to deliver effective training.

As stated in the previous section, there are three areas in which we must concentrate our effort to effectively and dramatically reduce the impact of the so-called human error in the bottom line of the regulated industries. For doing the right thing the first time, we need:

a. Better user-centered *documents* (working instructions, specifications, and procedures) with clear, complete, and comprehensive instructions

b. Better *training* to ensure that workers understand why they are doing what they are doing, why they always must follow instructions, and what happens when instructions are not followed

c. Better *supervision* to ensure that workers always follow procedures and working instructions while performing any function under a GMP-regulated environment

Steps to reduce human errors include:

- Addressing the conditions and reducing the stressors that increase the frequency of errors
- Designing facilities and equipment to prevent slips and lapses occurring or to increase the chance of detecting and correcting them

- Driving out complexity and designing jobs to avoid the need for tasks that involve very complex decisions, diagnoses, or calculations; for example, by writing procedures for rare events requiring decisions and actions
- Ensuring proper supervision particularly for inexperienced staff, or for tasks where there is a need for independent checking
- Checking that job aids such as procedures and instructions are clear, concise, available, up-to-date and accepted by users
- Considering the possibility of human error when undertaking risk assessments
- Thinking about the different causes of human errors during incident investigations in order to introduce measures to reduce the risk of a repeat incident
- Monitoring that measures taken to reduce error are effective
- Enhancing process (barrier) controls and poka-yokes
- Removing latent failures
- Making people accountable within a positive and blame-free environment toward errors and mistakes
- Understanding the hows and whys of human errors

To reduce violations managers could:

- Take steps to increase the chances of violations being detected using routine monitoring, internal audits and so on
- Make rules and procedure relevant and practical and eliminate unnecessary rules or instruction
- Train by explaining the reasons behind certain rules or procedures and their relevance
- Provide more training and better control (for example supervisory presence) for abnormal and emergency situations to minimize exceptional violations

We learned that lack of attention and lapse of memory play a significant role in all categories of human error. In regulated industries, these factors should be negligible because workers are not supposed to rely on memory for correct performance. Batch records, device master, and history files exist for a purpose. If you want to improve processes performed by humans at all levels, you must remember what Reason (1990) wrote:

- Fallibility is part of the human condition
- We can't change the human condition
- We can change the conditions under which people work
- Human beings will always make errors
- Naming, blaming, and shaming have no remedial value

Everyone can make errors no matter how well-trained and motivated they are. Sometimes we are "set up" by the system to fail. The challenge is to develop error-tolerant systems and to prevent errors from occurring.

Reducing human error involves far more than taking disciplinary action against an individual. There are a range of measures that provide more effective controls including design of the job and equipment, procedures, and training. Paying attention to individual attitudes and motivations, design features of the job and the organization will help to reduce violations. Table 5.3 contains recommendations for investigating human errors.

And last but not least important, we must establish an order for error control from best, ideal options to least effective barriers:

- Error or mistake proof: make the error impossible (computer form cannot be saved if some information is missed; microwave cannot operate if door is open; production tank will unlock and open only if scanned containers of ingredients matches the system's bill of material for this lot)

Table 5.3 Human error investigation and prevention Do's and Don'ts.

Do	Don't
• Investigate every human error up to its root cause(s) • Search for precursors of the human error (working from memory?) • Improve your working instructions and records by enhancing document format (imperative tone, graphic elements, clearn and comprehensive content) • Improve your training system • Measure the effectiveness of your training efforts	• Use human error as root cause • Use retraining as the default corrective action for human failures • Assume that your employees are lazy and careless about their jobs

- Error prevention: signals and alarms (red underline of incorrect spelling in Word)
- Minimize impact of error (inspection and test or double verification of the addition of components to a mixing tank)

6

Biggest Opportunities of the Investigation/CAPA System and How to Fix Them

This chapter describes a dozen of the most common opportunities or flaws of the investigation and CAPA system and how to fix them. Real examples from each opportunity are analyzed and best practices for each are discussed.

6.1 LACK OF INVESTIGATION PLAN

The investigation plan is probably the most important element of the investigation. However, you rarely can find this critical element in the investigation report. Most of the time, the investigation is an anarchic process full of back-and-forth, trial-and-error, or going-around-in-circles situations. As discussed in Chapter 4.2.5.1, a good investigation plan is essential to ensure that:

- The investigation is carried out methodically and in a professional manner
- Resources are used to best effect
- Focus is maintained
- Additional resources can be made available if required
- Potential root causes are not overlooked

While it is important that you start with a plan, investigations rarely proceed as originally predicted. You should therefore be ready to revise your plan, perhaps drastically, as new information emerges during the course of an investigation. Always follow the facts, rather than trying to make the facts fit into your plan. An investigation plan will define what you do, why you do it, and when you do it.

Of particular regulatory importance is the situation when the investigation plan includes performing additional tests. In such cases, a protocol should be prepared (subject to approval by the QCU) describing the additional testing to be performed and specifying the scientific and/or technical handling of the data. This is particularly important if your plan requires any test to material already on the market.

6.2 TIMELINESS (LACK OF)

There is tremendous variability regarding time frames the regulated companies establish to deal with several aspects of the CAPA system. These may range from no time limits (a rare occurrence) to 30-day limits (calendar or business), including the effectiveness check of corrective actions. The FDA has no requirement for time limits, mentioning only the term *reasonable* in a note published in 1997 as part of the Human Drug CGMP Notes by the Division of Manufacturing and Product Quality, Office of Compliance of the CDER:

> The CGMP regulations, at 21 CFR §211.192, establish the requirement for an investigation, but do not explicitly state a time interval for completing it, including the preparation of a report. Our expectation for "closure" of a failure investigation (including any other "unexplained discrepancy") is that the investigation be conducted and reported in a reasonable time. The *Barr* decision called this "timely" (see paragraph 23 of that decision).
>
> We see both the 30-day time period in the court decision and the 20-day time period in the referenced inspectional guide as being reasonable or timely; both are guidance and not requirements. The times differ because the Court addressed an investigation by a manufacturing site having a laboratory, whereas the guide addresses investigation in the laboratory only. We see the investigation in the manufacturing site that has a laboratory including other manufacturing aspects along with laboratory aspects.
>
> In discussing this topic, it may be helpful to point out what would not be reasonable, like performing an investigation but not progressing to a decision point as recorded in a final report/ decision document, delaying a decision on investigation findings beyond the expiration date of the lot(s) in question, or delaying/ excluding the investigation from GMP or application related records which require their inclusion.

When an investigation is reaching its self-imposed time limit, management often increases pressure on investigators and reviewers. The result is that most investigations are inadequately completed, but closed without exceeding the time limit. I enjoy asking during training sessions which is more important for management: closing on time or closing once the investigation is adequately completed. The honest response is always the same: on time. Returning to the time limit, we should differentiate among the three main stages of the Investigation/ CAPA system previously defined in Figure 4.2.

Investigation Stage

Typically, the investigation stage begins with the detection of an issue and extends until the probable root causes have been found. This stage is important because until we know the causes of the problem, everything is under suspicion. After an out-of-specification is observed during the test of an in-process material, components used for manufacture, personnel involved in the manufacture and analysis, and instruments and equipment used for manufacture are potential root causes that can be discarded only after the investigation has been performed. One of the first steps of any investigation is to establish whether the situation we are dealing with could be impacting other products or, even worse, our customers and patients. A typical example occurs when we discover an instrument out of calibration. In this situation, an assessment should be performed considering the worst case scenario: the equipment could have been out of tolerance since the last successful calibration, and all production material related to this equipment since then must be evaluated. This initial evaluation of the situation, based on the preliminary data and evidence available at this point, should be the first task when initiating any investigation. Details of the content of this initial impact assessment are discussed in Chapter 4.1.2.

Investigation of Best Practices

- Performing a risk assessment of the issue considering several risk factors (refer to Chapter 4.1.2). High-risk investigations will have priority over low-risk situations.
- Including a time frame for completing the investigation (from the date when the issue was discovered to the approval of the investigation). A reasonable time frame for this phase would be 20 calendar days for high-risk situations and 30 calendar days for medium-risk situations. Good investigations need time. Most corrections are implemented during this period, some of them even before the formal opening of the investigation.

CAPA Plan Stage

Once the root causes are identified, it is time to decide how we can avoid their recurrence. The best investigation can become a waste of effort if no adequate corrective actions are established and implemented. Unfortunately, most firms only develop and implement spot fixes. The

CAPA plan must consider the three main elements extensively covered in several other sections of this book:

a. Interim actions

b. Corrective actions

c. Preventive actions

CAPA Plan Best Practices

- Definitively, time is needed to analyze and develop effective corrective actions. Two weeks is a reasonable time frame to develop the CAPA plan.
- Avoid the use of "analyze," "evaluate," "assess," "investigate," or any synonym as corrective or preventive actions. Most of the time, such analysis and evaluation do not reach any further. It is one of the main reasons for the lack of real corrective and preventive action in our industry. These assessments (for example "evaluate whether any document must be changed") are performed during this CAPA plan time frame and their results (that is, "seven documents must be changed") is the true corrective or preventive action to be implemented. From a regulatory point of view, these assessments are part of the investigation phase. In other words, we need to extend our investigation to other products or processes that might have been impacted by the failure addressed through the current investigation.

Effectiveness Evaluation Stage

The time frame for this evaluation must be established case by case. Some firms establish a fixed period of time (one month, three months, and so on) for all effectiveness evaluations instead of correlating the period of time with the frequency of the process under evaluation. I have learned about a few companies that require completion of the entire Investigation and CAPA process within 30 days. This includes the investigation of the event to discover the root cause, the generation and implementation of corrective and preventive actions, and the evaluation of their effectiveness. Without question, these cases represent the poorest Investigation and CAPA systems I have seen, and the main factor is management's lack of understanding of the Investigation/CAPA system.

Effectiveness Evaluation Best Practices

Use the "double-digits" rule of thumb: Allow enough time to permit the evaluation of at least ten repetitions of the process under evaluation. If the process runs approximately every month, then one year could be a reasonable period of time to determine whether the corrective action was effective in avoiding the recurrence of the cause. If the process is performed weekly, then three months should be enough. For a daily process, one month is a good period of time to establish the effectiveness of a corrective action.

The rationale for this rule can be explained using a concept of reliability engineering called the Weibull distribution or, more commonly, the bathtub curve. A visual representation of the bathtub curve is presented in Figure 6.1.

As can be noticed from Figure 6.1, in the early stages of any change, the probability of failure is very high. As time elapses, the probability of failure decreases exponentially. This is what is called the "early failures period" or the "burn-in period." So, the first time we perform a task after any change, the probability of failure is very high, because we are still learning the new task. At this point in time, we need monitor the process very closely in order to avoid the probable failures inherent of this stage. The second stage of the bathtub curve shows what is called the "random failures period" or the "constant failures period." It is precisely in this region where we want to establish the time frame we will use to measure effectiveness, because in this region the probability of failure remains constant. So, for example, the probability of failure the 10th time we perform a task, must be the same as the probability of failure when we perform the task for the 15th, 20th, 25th, 30th time, and so on.

Finally, the last stage of the bathtub curve is called the "wear-out failures period." In this phase, if we do not provide frequent refreshers or training in our procedures, people can begin to start making slight changes in the way they perform the procedures that eventually lead to failures and nonconformances. So, in order to avoid the possible effects of the "wear-out failures period," an effective training and monitoring function must be established.

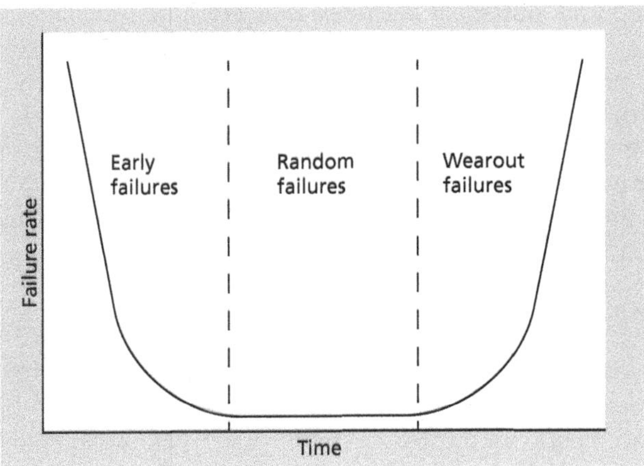

Figure 6.1 The Weibull distribution or bathtub curve.

6.3 EVERYTHING IS AN ISOLATED EVENT (LACK OF ADEQUATE TRENDING)

One of the first questions to be answered at the beginning of any investigation is fundamental: Is this the first time this situation happened? At this point of time, we only know symptoms: a lot failed a QC test or a customer complained about something. The answer to the question establishes the frequency or recurrence of the situation; it is one of the main elements of risk management within the investigation and CAPA process. If this is a recurrent issue, we already have a breakdown of our investigation and CAPA system because previous incidents were either not investigated or were not properly corrected.

Examples

Most companies do not have adequate procedures for trending and very often consider events to be isolated. Recent warning letters illustrate this situation:

> Failure to adequately establish and maintain procedures analyzing processes, work operations, concessions, quality audits reports, quality records, service records, complaints, returned product, and other sources of quality data to identify existing and potential causes of nonconforming product, or other quality problems, as required by 21 CFR §820.100(a)(1). For example, neither the Corrective and Preventive Action procedures, and Investigation Procedure nor the complaint handling procedure define the terms "trending" and "statistical methods." Defining trending and statistical methods assists in applying a consistent methodology in analyzing quality problems and adverse events. Trending and statistical methods that are not sufficiently robust may not be sensitive enough to detect significant increases in quality problems and adverse events. Furthermore, the complaint procedure indicates that quarterly trending of complaints will occur and links the trending to the CAPA procedure. However, neither procedure establishes when quarterly complaint analysis results are considered significant enough to warrant inclusion in the company CAPA subsystem.

Other examples:

> "In investigating this complaint, you considered it to be an isolated event and did not extend your investigation to product that had been distributed, even though you determined that the equipment X had been used on 93 lots from November 20,

> 20xx through January 23, 20xx, during the time when the operator involved in the complaint had been assigned to the sealing department. As this example illustrates, your firm has an established practice of considering only the number of complaints received, rather than the criticality of each complaint received, when determining whether there is a need to take preventative and / or corrective actions."
>
> "The CGMP deviations noted during the establishment inspection, where the firm's employees failed to follow Standard Operating Procedures, do not appear to be isolated events.... The commonality regarding the above referenced reworks is that the firm's requests stated that personnel training and experience were factors in the product quality as well as failure to follow Standard Operating Procedures."
>
> "Investigations of two positive sterility tests did not determine conclusive or probable root causes for the contamination. Although root causes were not determined, both investigations conclude that 'the impact of the sterility test positive was isolated to the affected batch' and all other batches placed on hold when the test failures were found were released for distribution."

Requirements for trending are scattered across the different regulations and were discussed in Chapter 4, focusing on the in-conformance analysis that constitutes the basis for preventive actions.

Best Practices

- Perform a search looking for indications of a previous event. This search must cover an adequate time frame and must be commensurate with the frequency of the process rather than a fixed period of time (for example, three or six months). In any case, be sure to evaluate at least the last ten times this process ran. Using this "double-digit" rule of thumb, if the frequency of the process is approximately every month, then one year should be a reasonable search period. If the process runs approximately every week, one quarter will be adequate.
- Always include the search query elements as part of the investigation. It's highly recommended that, as part of the review / approval process, someone should repeat the search query to verify its results. Few things are more dangerous to our credibility than an auditor finding that the "isolated" event was not so isolated.

6.4 ROOT CAUSE NOT IDENTIFIED

A common problem observed in many companies is that most nonconformance investigations point to human error or procedures not followed as the root cause of the nonconformity. As previously discussed, these are merely symptoms of deeper causes. To establish and maintain an effective investigation and CAPA system, companies must move beyond symptoms and causal factors and reach the root cause level of the problem.

This situation originated from the lack of an adequate root cause analysis process. Even though most regulated companies include many root cause tools within their investigation procedures, almost none of them require the use of the tools. It is like a wish list (tools you *could* use…). We need a root cause analysis system and management must enforce its use, not just suggest it. Training on root cause tools is not the usual main factor of a poor investigation. The main factor is the lack of application of the tools.

Examples

Following are typical examples of "root causes" that are merely symptoms:

- Human error
- Procedures not followed
- Equipment malfunction
- Improper performance
- Method not validated
- Multiple batches in process at the same time
- Clean-room gowns not used
- Equipment with expired calibration
- Result out of trend

Best Practices

- To correct this situation, the investigation and CAPA management team must avoid the use of any of the above-mentioned symptoms as root causes.
- In the above examples, ask *why* the point is out of trend or *why* the method was not validated.
- One of the best tools you can use is to ask *why* several times until you reach a fixable root cause.

Include the requirement to use problem-solving tools as part of your investigation procedure. I recommend including the following tools:

- Chronology
- Comparison matrix
- Cause-and-effect diagram
- Fault tree analysis

6.5 ROOT CAUSES IDENTIFIED BUT NOT CORRECTED

Always try to fix *all* the already identified root causes. Leaving "unattended" root causes today will create problems tomorrow. When you compare the root cause and the CAPA plan sections of any investigation report, very often they do not match. It is necessary to have at least one corrective action matched to every identified root cause.

Examples

The investigation report documented three root causes: lack of training, unclear document instructions, and inadequate supervision. Training and instructions were covered by corrective actions, but there was nothing related to the inadequate supervision.

Best Practices

- Do not follow the Pareto principle by fixing only the prominent cause
- Try to fix identified causes unless you can demonstrate a lack of risk

6.6 CORRECTING THE SYMPTOM INSTEAD OF THE CAUSE

Along with the abuse of human error and retraining (see Chapter 6.11), correcting the symptoms instead of the cause is perhaps the most prevalent investigation and CAPA problem experienced by regulated companies. Multiple causes can create this weakness of the investigation and CAPA system. I believe that most companies simply do not understand the differences between a correction (specific spot fix) and a corrective or preventive action (attack on the root cause). From operators to middle and top-level managers, all have a problem understanding key investigation and CAPA terms.

Examples

The following are simple corrections that are often disguised as corrective actions:

- Train a non-trained operator
- Reject and destroy a failing product
- Rework some nonconforming material
- Repair a piece of broken equipment
- Properly connect the alarm to the machine
- "Use as is" nonconforming products

Best Practices

- Ensure that your organization understands the meaning of and differences among correction, corrective action, and preventive action. Also be sure that workers can distinguish between symptoms and real root causes.
- Ensure there is at least a real and adequate corrective or preventive action for each identified root cause. Formulating a simple question can help you to differentiate between correction and corrective actions: Will this corrective action avoid (prevent) the cause occurring again? If the answer is no, then you have simply a correction.

6.7 LACK OF INTERIM ACTIONS

The need for interim corrective and/or preventive actions is one of the most unknown and unused concepts in the regulated industry. If a corrective action cannot be implemented immediately, then we must establish interim actions to avoid the recurrence of the situation while the permanent corrective action is implemented.

Reasons for delay in the implementation of the permanent action can be several and well-justified, including the need to buy and validate a piece of equipment or the need to change a written procedure. Inexcusable is the absence of some kind of interim action to cover the implementation period. Having no interim action in this situation is not acceptable. A worst-case scenario relates to those companies routinely allowing a very long period to elapse before implementing corrective and/or preventive actions. I have learned about a few of this kind, allowing nine months or even one full year to implement the corrective or preventive action. None of them used the interim action concept.

Examples

Several customer complaints were received due to missing components on a medical device kit. The current inspection is performed visually by packaging operators. The identified root cause was operator error due to visual fatigue, and the corrective action was to implement an electronic inspection system. The company allowed nine months for implementation of the new system. What interim control measures were established during those nine months? None. How many complaints were received during that period? Dozens. Interim actions this company could have taken include increasing sampling quantity or frequency and increasing inspection levels.

Another example occurs when a company has an open investigation, where the corrective or preventive actions are still in the process of being implemented. If the same root cause happens again, they would not open another investigation, but would add this incidence to the existing investigation. Consolidating the new occurrence under an open investigation is not so bad. However, the major problem here is that evidently no interim actions have been implemented to avoid the reoccurrence of the causes until the permanent action is implemented. Interim actions must avoid (or at least detect) the root cause until the permanent action is finally implemented.

Best Practices

Before you approve any action (especially corrective ones) always ask whether the process involving the nonconformance will be run again prior to the implementation of the corrective action. If the answer is yes, then you must request some interim action. Although interim actions must be specific to identified root causes, additional sampling or inspection and additional testing are among the most used. Another frequent example of an interim action is to use (by a planned deviation) a new version of a procedure that is still being routed for final approval.

6.8 LACK OF TRUE PREVENTIVE ACTIONS

Most CAPA systems are really only CA systems because they do not include preventive components. These companies are in the firefighting (corrective) mode and they lack the proactive approach that comes from the analysis of their *in-conformance* process results. Unfortunately, we must conclude that many regulated companies do not have a true CAPA system. The relationship between CA and PA establishes the maturity of the CAPA system.

Again, there is a lack of understanding of the differences between corrective action and preventive action. If the root cause is tied to a nonconformity, by definition the action to be taken must be corrective.

Other sources of true preventive actions are the FMEAs we discussed in Chapter 4.1.2 and the use of statistical process control, particularly the use of control charts. For example, in the FMEA, we identify the "potential" failure modes, the "potential" effects, and the "potential" causes. What *potential* means is that they have not happened yet. So, a mature risk management process must provide true preventive actions to our CAPA system, as defined in Chapter 4.5.3.1. The problem with most FMEAs, based on my experience, is that they are more reactive than proactive. Many companies try to answer the question "What has gone wrong?" instead of the question "What might go wrong?" Once companies start to use the FMEA in a proactive way, and establish links between FMEA and investigation and CAPA system, they will start implementing true preventive actions.

The same situation happens with the use of statistical process control. Many companies wait until they have out-of-control and out-of-specifications situations before doing anything. If used adequately, control charts can help us identify true preventive actions.

Chapter 8.6 includes examples of true preventive actions.

Best Practices

- Track and trend most significant processes based on risk.
- Monitor in-conformance results to identify developing adverse trends.
- Remember that preventive action deals with potential root causes.
- Consider other sources of preventive action such as management reviews, design reviews, and risk management reviews.
- Determine whether each corrective action can be implemented elsewhere as a preventive action (other systems, other products, and/or other processes).
- Do not use *evaluate, assess,* and *investigate* as preventive action.

6.9 LACK OF EFFECTIVENESS VERIFICATION OF THE ACTION TAKEN

A corrective action will be considered effective if it is able to avoid the recurrence of the cause. Therefore, the evaluation of the effectiveness cannot be tied to the presence or absence of the symptom, because:

- The same symptom can be produced by different root causes
- The same root cause can create different symptoms

There are also misunderstandings related to the verification of effectiveness. Some companies document that the action was implemented rather than provide evidence that the action worked as intended.

For those actions associated to training, we discussed the evaluation of training effectiveness in Chapter 4.4.2. From my experience, the two major flaws in the effectiveness verification are (1) that actions are not clear enough, and (2) the lack of adequate metrics. One way in which we analyze the effectiveness verification statements during our Investigation and CAPA Expert certification is to determine if those statements have these three elements: **A**ctions, **T**ime frame, and **M**etrics. We call it the ATM.

Examples of Inadequate Verification of Effectiveness

- The corrective action was implemented
- The problem did not appear during the past three months

Examples of Adequate Verification of Effectiveness

- During the next two months, a performance evaluation of 15 associates (five from each shift, randomly selected) will be performed to verify the use of personnel protective equipment. Corrective action will be considered effective if all evaluated operators were following the procedure.

It can be noticed that this effectiveness verification statement has actions (the performance evaluation), time frame (two months), and metrics (all operators follow the procedure).

Best Practices

- Clearly define the evaluation of the effectiveness of the corrective and/or preventive actions.
- Establish statistically sound verification plans, or at least use the "double-digits" rule of thumb: Allow enough time to permit the evaluation of at least ten repetitions of the process under evaluation.
  - If the process runs approximately every month, then one year should be a reasonable period of time to determine whether the corrective action was effective.
  - If the process is performed approximately every week, then three months should be enough.
  - For a daily process, one month is a good period of time to establish effectiveness.

6.10 MULTIPLE CAPA SYSTEMS WITHOUT CORRELATION

Companies must identify and document relevant data sources or feeders of the CAPA system. The sources are both internal and external to the company, and the company must integrate those data sources and data elements in order to identify rising issues or developing adverse patterns.

Often this analysis is segmented by geography (domestic versus international) or other factors. The disastrous result is that no one in the organization can see the whole CAPA system picture.

Examples of Inspection Findings

- Firm's management of corrective and preventive actions (CAPA) is inadequate. Specifically, the firm is taking CAPAs under various quality data headings (incidences, nonconformities) without correlation into the firm's CAPA system, preventing accurate analysis and timely review.
- Two databases are used to handle complaints (domestic (US) and international), with the result that management is made aware only of some complaints received.
- Corrective and preventive actions generated from internal audit observations are not included in the general CAPA database; therefore, they are not evaluated during management review meetings.

Best Practices

- Have only one Investigation and CAPA system.
- Establish meaningful metrics and tracking processes for your Investigation and CAPA system.
- Do not forget to analyze your Investigation/CAPA system by root cause categories.
- Compare and evaluate key Investigation/CAPA metrics with your sister facilities.

6.11 ABUSE OF HUMAN ERROR AND RETRAINING

Even though this topic was discussed in Chapter 5.6, we want to include some remarks here:

- Between 80 and 90 percent of corrective and preventive actions taken in the regulated industries are related to humans working with their processes.
- Human error is not a root cause; it is simply a symptom of a more profound cause.
- Humans are involved in all processes and fallibility is part of the human condition. Humans will always make errors.
- We can't change the human condition, but we can change the conditions under which humans work.

Examples

Here are some examples of working instructions not followed by operators. In all related nonconformance investigations, the root cause was assigned to "operator error." You will notice that with these instructions, anybody will fail:

- Verify all parameters
- Mix well
- Mix slowly
- As soon as possible
- Mix for a minimum of 30 minutes
- Stick together for a few seconds

Best Practices

- There is only one: Do not use human error as a root cause. Always ask *why* the human made the mistake.

6.12 FOCUSING MORE ON THE SOFTWARE THAN ON THE INVESTIGATION AND CAPA SYSTEM

During some of our training sessions, participants often express their frustration with the system they use to document their nonconformances, failure investigations, corrective/preventive actions, and the verification of effectiveness of those actions. When something like this happens, they really lose sight of the importance of having a structured approach for the investigation and CAPA system. They struggle more with how to make the system work than with the genuine importance of things like identifying all the probable root causes, identifying corrective and/or preventive actions, implementing these actions, and verifying their effectiveness.

Examples

- "My software only allows me to select one root cause."
- "Human error is one of the root causes to select from the root causes drop-down menu."
- "My system does not have a field in which I can document corrections; it only provides for corrective and preventive actions."

Best Practices

- Perform a thorough assessment of your needs before installing any software.
- Make the software work for you, not vice versa.
- Do not include elements such as "human error," "procedure not followed," "equipment malfunction," or "other" in your root cause categories drop-down menus.

7

Developing an Internal Investigation and CAPA Expert Certification

To enhance your investigation and CAPA system, it is highly recommended that you certify your investigators, CAPA owners, and investigation/CAPA reviewers and approvers. As an example, we are including the investigation and CAPA expert certification model our company has developed.

7.1. CONTENT OF THE CERTIFICATION

The investigation and CAPA system certification (see Tables 7.1 to 7.5) is a comprehensive certification course consisting of six elements with a total duration of five days equivalent to 35 contact hours. Approximately 30 percent of this time is be devoted to practice exercises. This certification covers the following five areas:

- Problem detection
- Problem description
- Root cause analysis
- CAPA plan
- Effectiveness evaluation

Upon completion of this certification program, participants will be able to:

- Write effective investigation reports
- Identify the major opportunities of their investigation and CAPA system
- Evaluate the investigation process to identify root causes
- Apply effective corrective and preventive actions that will avoid the recurrence or occurrence of the causes
- Measure the effectiveness of the actions implemented

Our company, Business Excellence Consulting Inc. (BEC), is accredited by the International Association for Continuing Education and Training (IACET). BEC complies with the ANSI/IACET Standard, which is recognized internationally as a standard of excellence in instructional practices. As a result of this accreditation, BEC is authorized to issue the IACET CEU (3.5 CEUs) for this program. Full attendance to the learning event is mandatory to receive CEUs.

The detailed content of each module is described in tables 7.1 to 7.5. A syllabus of this certification is included in the companion CD.

Table 7.1 Investigation and CAPA expert certification day 1.

CAPA System Expert Certification (Day 1)	
Agenda	
8:30–9:30	**Opening Remarks and Pre-Test**
9:30–10:15	**Introduction** • The Vicious Cycle • The Correct CAPA Flow • Root Cause Identification • The Closed-Loop CAPA Process
10:15–10:30	**Break**
10:30–12:00	**CAPA and the Regulations** • Adulteration • CAPA in the Pharmaceutical Industry • CAPA in the Medical Devices Industry • The CAPA Link Between Pharmaceutical and Medical Devices • Main FDA Findings • Eleven Opportunities of the CAPA System
12:00–13:00	**Lunch**
13:00–14:30	**QSIT: Auditing the CAPA System** • Purpose and Importance of the CAPA System • CAPA Inspectional Objectives
14:30–15:00	**Current Regulatory Trends** • Top Observations in the Pharmaceutical Industry • Top Observations in the Medical Device Industry • CAPA Subsystem Warning Letters Summary
15:00–15:15	**Break**
15:15–17:00	**Risk Management and CAPA** • Regulatory Requirements • The Risk-Based Matrix • Integration of Risk Management and CAPA • A Systematic Approach

Table 7.2 Investigation and CAPA expert certification day 2.

CAPA System Expert Certification (Day 2)	
Agenda	
8:30–9:00	**Introduction**
9:00–10:15	**Elements of an Investigation Report** • Event Information • Description of the Issue • Immediate Actions Taken • Initial Impact Assessment • Investigation Details • Conclusions About Root Causes • CAPA Plan • Final Disposition and Approval • Executive Summary
10:15–10:30	**Break**
10:30–12:00	**Problem Solving Methodology** • Focus of the Model • Defining the Problem • Chronological Analysis • Change Analysis • Searching for Trends • Flowchart
12:00–13:00	**Lunch**
13:00 –15:00	**Problem Solving Methodology (cont.)** • Is/Is Not Matrix • Problem Definition Case Study • Barrier Control Analysis • Causal Factor and Root Cause Identification
15:00–15:15	**Break**
15:15–16:00	**Root Cause Analysis Tools** • Fishbone • 5 Whys • Fault Tree Analysis
16:00–17:00	**Final Thoughts** • How to Investigate Human Errors • Root Cause Categories

Table 7.3 Investigation and CAPA expert certification day 3.

CAPA System Expert Certification (Day 3)	
Agenda	
8:30–9:00	**Introduction**
9:00–10:15	**Elements of the CAPA Plan** • Corrections • Corrective Actions • Preventive Actions • Generating Corrective and Preventive Actions • Effectiveness Evaluation
10:15–10:30	**Break**
10:30–12:00	**Twelve Biggest CAPA Opportunities** • Lack of Investigation Plan • Timeliness • Everything is an Isolated Event • Root Cause Not Identified • Correcting the Symptoms Instead of the Cause
12:00–13:00	**Lunch**
13:00–15:00	**Twelve Biggest CAPA Opportunities (cont.)** • Lack of Interim Corrective Actions • Root Cause Identified but Not Corrected • Lack of True Preventive Actions • Lack of Effectiveness Verification of Action Taken • Multiple CAPA Systems Without Correlation • Abuse of Human Error and Retraining • Over-Customization of the CAPA System
15:00–15:15	**Break**

Table 7.4 Investigation and CAPA expert certification day 4.

CAPA System Expert Certification (Day 4)	
Agenda	
8:30–9:00	**Introduction**
9:00–10:15	**Human Errors and Human Factors** • Key Points to Consider • From Human Error to Defect • Dealing with Human Errors • Types of Human Failures • Memory Slips and Lapses • Attention, Memory, and Human Errors • Latent Failures and Human Factors Natural Mappings
10:15–10:30	**Break**
10:30–11:15	**Investigating Human Errors** • Causal Factor and Root Cause Identification • How to Investigate Human Errors • Interviewing, Not Interrogating • Human Error Investigation Form • Human Error Investigation Key Points
11:15–12:00	**Human Error and Retraining** • Training as Human Factor • How to Reduce the Probability of Human Errors • Human Errors and Memory • Areas to Focus
12:00–13:00	**Lunch**
13:00–13:45	**Technical Writing:** Measures of Excellence
13:45–14:30	• Documentation Style Manual o Grammar and Correct and Preferred Usage of Words
14:30–15:00	**Sentence Construction:** Imperative Sentences and Active versus Passive Sentences
15:00–15:15	**Break**
15:15–17:00	**Writing Effective Documents** • Writing Styles • Executive Summary • The Technical Writing Process o Planning and Organizing the Document o The Outline o Drafting Documents o Revising-Editing Documents and Proofreading o Things to Avoid: Alarm Words • Writing for Effectiveness: Clarity, Economy, Readability, and Correctness • Good Writing Practices

Table 7.5 Investigation and CAPA expert certification day 5.

CAPA System Expert Certification (Day 5)	
Agenda	
8:30–9:00	**Regulatory Importance of Statistical Process Control** • Process Control within the Code of Federal Regulation, FDA Guidances, and International Guidances & Standards
9:00–9:15	**SPC and the Life Sciences Regulated Industry** • Recent Observations about Misuse of Statistical Process Control
9:15–9:45	**Process Variation** • The Causes of Variation
9:45–10:15	**Basic Principles about Statistics** • Descriptive Statistics • The Importance of Descriptive Statistics • The Importance of Addressing Normality of the Data
10:15–10:30	**Break**
10:30–11:00	**Graphical Tools** • Describing the Data: Histogram and Dot Plot • Comparing Groups: Box Plot • Prioritizing Our Actions: Pareto Diagram • Analyzing Relationships: Scatter Plot • Time is an Important Consideration • Looking for Non-Randomness: Run Chart
11:00–11:30	**Process Capability** • Analyzing Process Capability • Process Capability Indices • Process Capability Example
11:30–12:00	**Control Charts** • Types of Control Charts • Control Chart Selection • Variables Control Charts • Attributes Control Charts
12:00–13:00	**Lunch**
13:00–14:00	**Final Thoughts**
14:00–14:45	**Training Wrap Up and Test Review**
14:45–15:00	**Break**
15:00–17:00	**Post-Test**

7.2 EVALUATING THE EFFECTIVENESS OF INVESTIGATION AND CAPA TRAINING EFFORTS

The objective of this evaluation is to be able to demonstrate (using objective evidence) that the training efforts are effective. A comprehensive training effectiveness evaluation system is conducted using the four levels of the Kirkpatrick model through the use of the following materials for each phase of the model:

- **Reaction (level 1):** an evaluation form at the end of the training, covering issues such as material's organization, trainer's knowledge about the topics, and training environment.
- **Learning (level 2):** a pre-test prior to the beginning of the training, plus a post-test at the end of the training. A minimum grade of 70% in the post-test is required to pass the certification.
- **Behavior (level 3):** the submission of an existing CAPA investigation report, red-lined with all the deficiencies found by applying all the knowledge acquired during the training.
- **Results (level 4):** the company might be able to measure the results of this certification process by analyzing pre- and post-certification metrics such as amount of CAPA investigations opened, time to complete CAPA investigations, and recurrence of the issues that cause a CAPA investigation, among others. A downward trend in all these metrics is expected.

The evaluation (level 3) of each investigation report is accomplished using the investigation and CAPA assessment forms included in Chapter 8.4. The elements of the evaluation are described in Table 7.6.

Table 7.6 Investigation and CAPA expert certification evaluation levels.

Elements of Certification
a. Prerequisites: minimal experience requirements and internal training
b. Evaluation of training effectiveness
1. **Reaction** (survey after training)
2. **Learning** (exam: pre- and post-training)
3. **Behavior** (by instructor, evaluating investigations realized by each candidate to certification)
4. **Results** (measured by sponsor and certification instructor, based on pre-established metrics)
c. Recertification process: good *Investigation and CAPA practices* annual refresher

8

Documenting Investigation and CAPA: Forms and Examples

8.1 CONTENT OF THE INVESTIGATION REPORT

The investigation report should include the following elements:

PROBLEM DESCRIPTION

- Affected product / process / system
- Date / time occurred (if known)
- Date / time discovered
- Date / time reported
- What happened?
- What should have happened? (What is the specification, or instruction?)
- Where did it happen?
- How and where was the event discovered?
- Who discovered it?

IMMEDIATE ACTIONS TAKEN

- What was done after the situation was discovered?

INITIAL IMPACT ASSESSMENT

- Does this situation impact other products, equipment, raw materials, components, and / or systems?
- If there is product involved in this investigation, identify and evaluate lots or batches run before and / or after the event under investigation

- Has any affected material already been released / distributed to customers?
- Risk classification of the event

INVESTIGATION PLAN

- Describe the proposed investigation plan

INVESTIGATION DETAILS

- Problem definition
  - Background and historical data (trend analysis)
  - Chronology of the event
  - Comparison matrix (Is-Is Not)
- Current barrier analysis
- Root cause analysis
  - Causal factors
  - Potential root causes
    - Cause-and-effect diagram
    - Fault tree analysis

CONCLUSION ABOUT ROOT CAUSES

- What are the most probable root cause(s) of this situation?
- Root cause classification

FINAL DISPOSITION—APPROVAL OF INVESTIGATION

- What is the final decision taken regarding the affected product / process / system?
- Approval signatures

EXECUTIVE SUMMARY/ABSTRACT

Provide a short summary of the investigation facts and results, including a description of the event and the list of correction, corrective and/or preventive actions taken.

Note: comparison matrix and fault tree analysis may not be necessary for all investigations but their use is highly recommended.

8.2 CONTENT OF THE CAPA PLAN

The CAPA Plan should include the following elements:

a. **Correction/Containment Action(s)**
b. **Corrective Action.** Must have at least one identified CA for each root cause already identified. Each corrective action must include the following information:
    - How this action will avoid the recurrence of the identified root causes
    - Recommended interim action, if the proposed CA is not immediate
    - Implementation verification: how, when, and by whom
    - Effectiveness check: how, when, and by whom
    - Can this action be extended to other products/processes/systems not yet affected by this root cause? If yes, open a preventive action
c. **Preventive Action.** Should have at least one identified PA for each potential root cause already identified. Each preventive action must include the following information:
    - How this action will avoid the occurrence of the identified potential root causes
    - Recommended interim action, if the proposed PA is not immediate
    - Implementation verification: how, when, and by whom
    - Effectiveness check: how, when, and by whom

8.3 COMPLIANCE WRITING

Table 8.1 contains some basic recommendations to be followed when writing a compliance report. The list of Don'ts to be avoided when writing investigation reports or some other type of CAPA documents is long. The first recommendation is to avoid passion. Investigation reports in particular and regulatory documents in general must state facts and data only. Speculations, perceptions, and opinions do not have a place in the compliance writing world.

Following are some examples taken from real investigation reports. Certainly there are more than facts and data in these phrases:

"This product is *always* running on the low side of the specifications"

"...this was an *extremely* low failure..."

"Two *consecutive* lots gave OOS very high"

"...Due to *noncompliance* with batch record instructions"

"This product is *always* running *very close* to the lower specification limit"

"Assessment time exceeded: Situation was reported but assessment was not completed on the two-day period required *due to multiple priorities in the area*"

"After a *while,* the recorder..."

"This was a *real* isolated incident..."

"This extension of CAPA number...is necessary because the CAPA owner will be on vacations the next two weeks"

Table 8.1 Compliance writing Do's and Don'ts.

Do	Don't
Clarity	• Use inflammatory statements
• Use concrete and specific words	• Be judgmental
• Use active verbs	• Assign blame
• Use standard English words	• Speculate about liabilities or lack of compliance
• Be positive	• Make a broad conclusion
Readability	• Offer unsupported opinions, perceptions, and speculations
• Replace long words with short words	• Make personal references
• Break long sentences	• Use loaded words
Economy	• Sensationalize (this was a *critical* failure)
• Cut empty verbs	• Use unnecessary details
• Cut unnecessary prepositions	• Guess
• Cut redundancy	• Exaggerate
Correctness	• Be imprecise
• Check word choice	• Use absolutes such as always, ever, or totally
• Check grammar	• Use alarm words such as bad, catastrophic, critical failure, or negligent
• Check punctuation	
• Proofread	

8.4 FORMS

The following six forms are provided in this Chapter and they are also included in the companion CD in editable (Microsoft Word) format:

8.4.1. *Investigation Report.* It includes all details that must be included as part of the investigation, from the description of the event to the conclusion of the most probable root causes. It includes the Investigation plan.

8.4.2. *Root Cause Analysis checklist.* It includes all categories and subcategories described in Chapter 4.2.6

8.4.3. *Human Error Investigation.* This form is recommended to be used when human error is the apparent causal factor of the event. The form allows discovery of potential precursors or hidden human factors that can be associated with the situation under investigation.

8.4.4. *CAPA Plan.* This includes corrections, corrective actions, and preventive actions and the evaluation of their implementation and effectiveness.

8.4.5. *Investigation Report Assessment.* This form is recommended for the reviewer when documenting the merits of an investigation including attachment evaluation and overall writing effectiveness. It is also recommended for the investigator when a self-assessment of the investigation is made.

8.4.6. *CAPA Plan Assessment.* This form is recommended for the reviewer when documenting the merits of a CAPA plan including attachment evaluation and overall writing effectiveness. It is also recommended for the CAPA owner when a self-assessment of the CAPA plan is made.

8.4.1 Investigation Report

Table 8.2 Investigation report.

Problem Description	
Affected Product/Process/System	
Date/time occurred	
Date/time discovered	
Date/time reported	
What happened?	
What should have happened? (What is the specification or instruction?)	
Where did it happen?	
How the situation was discovered?	
Where the situation was discovered?	
Who discovered it?	
What type of defect does this situation represent?	

Immediate Action(s) Taken	
What have been done after discovery of the event to fix/contain it?	
Initial Impact Assesment	
Describe if this situation impacts other products, equipment, raw materials, components and/or systems	
If there is product involved in this event, identify and evaluate lots/batches run before and/or after the event under investigation	
Identify if any affected material is already released/distributed to customers	
Risk of the event	

(Continued)

(Continued)

Table 8.2 Investigation report.

Investigation Plan	
Investigation Plan Proposed	

Investigation Details	
Background and Historical data (Trend Analysis)	
Chronology of the event	
Current Barrier Analysis	
Causal Factor(s)	
Potential Root Cause(s)	
Cause and Effect Diagram	
Other Problem Solving Tools such as is/is not diagram, fault tree analysis and so on	

Conclusion About Root Cause(s)	
What is (are) the most probable root cause(s) of this situation? Describe.	
Root cause classification	

Final Disposition/Approval	
Final decision taken regarding the affected Product/Process/System	
Required approval signatures	

8.4.2 Root Cause Analysis Checklist

Table 8.3 Root cause analysis checklist.

	Subcategory	Ruled-In	Ruled-Out	Comments
Personal Performance	Lack of attention (inattention to details, working from memory)			
	Continuous attitude problems			
	Fatigue			
	Lack of capability (sensory, physical, intellectual)			
	Personal problems			
	Medication problems			

	Subcategory	Ruled-In	Ruled-Out	Comments
Training	Training not required			
	Missing training			
	Content not adequate			
	Training method not adequate			
	Language barriers			
	Environment not adequate			
	Instructor not adequate			
	Insufficient practice			
	Frequency not adequate			

(Continued)

(Continued)

Table 8.3 Root cause analysis checklist.

	Subcategory	Ruled-In	Ruled-Out	Comments
Equipment	Inadequate or defective design			
	Inadequate installation or validation			
	Historical lack of reliability			
	Equipment not included in maintenance program			
	Inadequate corrective maintenance			
	Inadequate preventive maintenance			
	Equipment not calibrated			
	Calibration failure			
	Missing equipment			
	Incorrect utilization of equipment			

	Subcategory	Ruled-In	Ruled-Out	Comments
Human Reliability Factors	Inadequate location of equipment			
	Inadequate identification of equipment, material, and so on			
	Cluttered or inadequate layout			
	Inadequate environmental conditions (cold, hot, poor illumination and so on)			
	Inadequate housekeeping			
	Stress condition (rush)			
	Excessive workload			
	Excessive calculation or data manipulation			
	Multitasking			

(Continued)

(Continued)

Table 8.3 Root cause analysis checklist.

Procedures and Instruction / Task Design	Subcategory	Ruled-In	Ruled-Out	Comments
	Lack of procedures or instructions			
	Procedure not required to use			
	Procedure not available or difficult to obtain			
	Procedure difficult to use			
	Procedure ambiguous or confusing			
	Lack of sufficient details			
	Document format not adequate			
	Incomplete instructions			
	Wrong instruction			
	Typographical error			
	Obsolete document			
	Document not approved			

Supervision and Management	Subcategory	Ruled-In	Ruled-Out	Comments
	Verbal instructions/ communication problems			
	Inadequate communication between shifts			
	Inadequate supervision			
	Improper allocation of resources (lack of personnel)			

(Continued)

(Continued)

Table 8.3 Root cause analysis checklist.

	Subcategory	Ruled-In	Ruled-Out	Comments
Materials	Inadequate storage conditions			
	Inadequate sampling instructions			
	Material not adequate (used while hold or quarantined)			
	Inadequate material substitution			
	Shipping damage			
	Marginal material			
	Specification not appropriate			
	Marginal supplier			
	Supplier not approved			

	Subcategory	Ruled-In	Ruled-Out	Comments
Environment	Inadequate pest control			
	Unfavorable environmental conditions			

8.4.3 Human Error Investigation

Table 8.4 contains 50 questions that can be used as guidance during the investigation of human errors. The purpose of these questions is to obtain a better understanding of the human factors surrounding the issue under investigation. It is not a mere checklist and it must be used along with regular root cause analysis tools such as cause-and-effect diagrams and fault tree analysis.

Table 8.4 Human error investigation.

Topic	Objective Evidence
Procedure Quality and Content	
1. Is there a formal (written) instruction to perform this task?	
2. Were procedures or working instructions available in the immediate area where the task was performed?	
3. Did the procedure or working instruction change recently?	
4. Is the procedure or working instruction clear and well understood by the employee?	
5. Does the procedure or working instruction have sufficient level of detail?	
6. Did the procedure or working instruction use specific details rather than a qualitative description (slowly, soon, few, well, and so on)?	
7. Can procedures or working instructions be considered adequate in terms of format, content, level of details, and so on?	
8. Are procedures or working instructions clearly written and without ambiguity in what is required?	
9. Does the employee need to perform processing or interpretation of the information to execute this task?	

(Continued)

(Continued)

Table 8.4 Human error investigation.

10. Does the employee clearly understand the applicable procedure or working instruction?	
11. Is there consistency in how employees are performing this task?	
12. Is the error related to numbers or alphanumeric information (for example, specifications, batch numbers, and so on)?	
13. Is there any barrier(s) in place to specifically avoid this failure?	
General	
14. Did the employee miss the task (omission error)?	
15. If this was a documentation omission, is the record designed to easily identify omissions?	
16. Did the employee erroneously perform the task (commission error)?	
17. Does the task require the employee to follow a specific sequence of steps?	
18. Did the employee read the procedure or work instruction while executing the task?	
19. Is there any job aids or checklist to perform this task? a. Are their format/content appropriate for clear interpretation? b. Did the employee use the job aid(s)?	
20. Review the procedure or working instruction with the employee and verify current practices against written instructions.	
21. Did the employee work from memory while executing this task?	

(Continued)

(Continued)

Table 8.4 Human error investigation.

22. Does this task include a second person verification or checking?	
23. What reason did the employee provide to justify this error?	
Training	
24. Was the employee formally and properly trained on the task or procedure?	
25. How was the employee trained on this task? (Describe the training method.)	
26. Does the training cover this specific task?	
27. What was the length of the training for this specific task?	
28. Who trained this employee?	
29. Who trained the other employees who did the task correctly?	
Layout/Conditions	
30. Was the employee working on "autopilot" because he/she is very familiar with the task?	
31. Was the employee performing any other task concurrently (multitasking)?	
32. Does the task require processing too much information or focusing on too many things at the same time?	
33. Are other tasks interrupting the performance of this task?	
34. Was the area's layout or workspace overcrowded?	
35. Is the area disorganized, causing employees to have to move around to perform tasks?	

(Continued)

(Continued)

Table 8.4 Human error investigation.

36. Were working conditions comfortable? (Noise, temperature, humidity, illumination, well-lit with bright light, and so on.)	
37. Was the person tired?	
38. Is the system design/layout consistent with regular human conventions?	
39. Was the supervisor or group leader present when the error occurred?	
40. Did the error occur during overtime?	
41. Did the error occur prior to or after a break or shift change?	
42. Did the error occur prior to or after a shutdown or vacation period?	
43. Was it a situation of competing priorities?	
44. Was it a situation of very tight deadline?	
45. Was it a situation of resource shortage?	
46. When exactly did the error occur? (Be precise.)	
Trends	
47. Is this the first time the employee performed this task? a. If it's not the first time, when was the last time he/she performed this task? b. If it's not the first time, how often does the employee perform this task?	
48. How many other employees do the same task correctly under the same conditions?	
49. Has the employee performed the task correctly earlier?	
50. How often did this (or similar) error occur during the last year?	

8.4.4 CAPA Plan

Table 8.5 CAPA plan.

CAPA Plan—Correction	
Correction/Containment/Remedial action(s) already taken	
Additional Correction/Containment/ Remedial action(s) that must be taken	

CAPA Plan—Corrective Action #1[1]	
Corrective Action for root cause #1	
How this action will avoid the **recurrence** of the identified root cause?	
If the proposed CA is not immediate, provide interim action(s)	
Implementation Verification: how, when and by whom	
Effectiveness Check: how, when and by whom	
Can this action be extended to other product/process/system not yet affected by this root cause? If yes, open a Preventive Action	

CAPA Plan—Preventive Action #1[1]	
Preventive Action for root cause #1	
How this action will avoid the **occurrence** of the identified potential root cause?	
If the proposed PA is not immediate, what are interim action(s)?	
Implementation Verification: how, when and by whom	
Effectiveness Check: how, when and by whom	

[1] Replicate this section as needed

8.4.5 Investigation Report Assessment

Table 8.6 Investigation report assessment.

Investigation Report No.	
Review completed by/date	
Additional documents reviewed	
Main comments	

Criteria	Yes	No	Comments
PROBLEM DESCRIPTION Does the report clearly describe:			
Affected Product/Process/System:			
Date/time occurred			
Date/time discovered			
Date/time reported			
What happened?			
What should have happened? (What is the specification or instruction?)			
Where did it happened?			
How the situation was discovered?			
Where the situation was discovered?			
Who discovered it?			
What type of defect does this situation represent?			

(Continued)

(Continued)

Table 8.6 Investigation report assessment.

Criteria	Yes	No	Comments
IMMEDIATE ACTION(S) TAKEN Does the report clearly describe:			
What has been done after discovery of the event to fix/contain it			
INITIAL IMPACT ASSESSMENT Does the report clearly describe:			
Does this situation impact other products, equipment, raw materials, components and/or systems?			
If there is product involved in this event, identify and evaluate lots/ batches ran before and/or after the event under investigation			
Are any affected material already released/distributed to customers?			
Risk of the event			

Criteria	Yes	No	Comments
INVESTIGATION PLAN Does the report clearly describe:			
Investigation Plan Proposed			

(Continued)

(Continued)

Table 8.6 Investigation report assessment.

Criteria	Yes	No	Comments
INVESTIGATION DETAILS Does the report clearly describe:			
Background and Historical data (Trend Analysis)			
Chronology of the event			
Current Barrier Analysis			
Causal Factor(s)			
Potential Root Cause(s)			
Cause and Effect Diagram			
Other Problem Solving Tools such as is/is not diagram, fault tree analysis and so on			

Criteria	Yes	No	Comments
CONCLUSION ABOUT ROOT CAUSE(S) Does the report clearly describe:			
What is (are) the most probable root cause(s) of this situation?			
Root cause classification?			

Criteria	Yes	No	Comments
FINAL DISPOSITION/ APPROVAL Does the report clearly describe:			
Does the report clearly describe the final decision taken regarding the affected Product/Process/System?			
Does he report contains adequate approval signatures?			

(Continued)

(Continued)

Table 8.6 Investigation report assessment.

Criteria	Yes	No	Comments
ATTACHMENT(S)			
Are the attachment(s) appropriately identified?			
Are all the attachments necessary?			
Does the attachment(s) include COMPLETE information?			

Overall Writing Effectiveness			
Criteria	**Yes**	**No**	**Comments**
Does the report:			
Contain **Clear Narrative** (does it stands alone without the author "interpreting" it)?			
Contain **Concise Narrative** (to the point)?			
Follow a **Logical Flow** (any educated reviewer or auditor can follow it and understand)?			
Provide **objective evidence** to support conclusions?			
Contain an **impersonal "tone"** without opinions, guessing or passions? (Only facts and objective data!)			

Additional Comments

8.4.6 CAPA Plan Assessment

Table 8.7 CAPA plan assessment.

CAPA Plan No.	
Review completed by/date	
Additional Documents Reviewed	
Main Comments	

Criteria	Yes	No	Comments
CAPA PLAN—CORRECTION Does the report clearly describe:			
Correction/Containment/Remedial action(s) already taken			
Additional Correction/Containment/ Remedial action(s) that must be taken			

Criteria	Yes	No	Comments
CAPA PLAN—CA Does the report clearly describe:			
At least one identified CA for each root cause already identified?			
How this action will avoid the recurrence of the identified root cause?			
If the proposed CA is not immediate, does it provide any interim action(s)?			
Implementation Verification: how, when and by whom?			
Effectiveness Check: how, when and by whom?			
Can this action be extended to other product/process/system not yet affected by this root cause? If yes, was a Preventive Action opened?			

(Continued)

(Continued)

Table 8.7 CAPA plan assessment.

Criteria	Yes	No	Comments
CAPA PLAN—PA Does the report clearly describe:			
At least one identified PA for each potential root cause already identified?			
How this action will avoid the occurrence of the identified root cause?			
If the proposed PA is not immediate, does it provide any interim action(s)?			
Implementation Verification: how, when and by whom?			
Effectiveness Check: how, when and by whom?			

Criteria	Yes	No	Comments
ATTACHMENT(S)			
Are the attachment(s) appropriately identified?			
Are all the attachments necessary?			
Does the attachment(s) include COMPLETE information?			

(Continued)

(Continued)

Table 8.7 CAPA plan assessment.

Overall Writing Effectiveness			
Criteria	Yes	No	Comments
Does the CAPA Plan report:			
Contains **Clear Narrative**? (Does it stands alone without the author "interpreting" it?)			
Contains **Concise Narrative** (to the point)?			
Follows a **Logical Flow** (any educated reviewer or inspector can follow it and understand)?			
Provides **objective evidence** to support conclusions?			
Contains an **impersonal "tone"** without opinions, guessing or passions? (Only facts and objective data!)			

Additional Comments

8.5 EXAMPLES OF INVESTIGATION REPORTS

This is an example of a ***deficient*** investigation and CAPA plan.

PROBLEM DESCRIPTION

Company ABC's Customer Service Center received numerous complaints during the past few weeks. All complaints were related to packaging defects for the 250 mg tablets of the Cherry Flavored product.

IMMEDIATE ACTION(S) TAKEN

After the customer complaints were received, the current lot of Cherry Flavored 500 mg tablets was observed. Twenty finished bottles were inspected and the defect was not found on any of them. So, this is considered an isolated event.

INVESTIGATION DETAILS

Company ABC manufactures chewable tablets to treat headaches. The company is established since January 2001. The facility is located in Town City (USA) and produces the drug in six different presentations: Cherry Flavored 250 mg, Grape Flavored 250 mg, Lemon Flavored 250 mg, Cherry Flavored 500 mg, Grape Flavored 500 mg, and Lemon Flavored 500 mg. There are five non-dedicated packaging lines; that is, any line can handle any one of the six presentations. The product is distributed in the U.S. East Coast.

The plant operates three shifts. The first shift currently has the most senior employees, while the third shift has the most recent employees. The new employees are on a "learning curve" during their first three months working directly with the first-shift operators. After that period, they start to work on their shift, without any direct input from their trainers. Company ABC experienced a massive hiring of employees during the period of FEB-01-2015 to MAY-31-2015.

The company has been receiving customer complaints since MAY-01-2015 due to product mix up on lot #ABC-01234. In Florida, 25 complaints were received for the Cherry Flavored 250 mg mixed with Grape Flavored 250 mg. In North Carolina, there were 26 customer complaints for the Cherry Flavored 250 mg mixed with Grape Flavored 250 mg. In New York, 48 complaints were received for the Cherry Flavored 250 mg mixed with Grape Flavored 250 mg.

CONCLUSION ABOUT ROOT CAUSE(S)

After gathering information, it can be concluded that the failure was due to a human error. The failure was probably caused by the new operators hired in 01-FEB-2015, because the customer complaints were received immediately after the new operators started to work alone on their shift.

CAPA PLAN:

Retrain all the operators in the third shift to be more cautious when they are working in order to avoid the occurrence of the failure in the future.

FINAL DISPOSITION

After completing the investigation process, it was determined that since it is an isolated event, no other action need to be taken. The investigation was closed on JUN-10-2015.

Now, this is an *improved* version of the same investigation and CAPA plan.

EXECUTIVE SUMMARY:

Company ABC's Customer Service Center received 99 complaints from MAY-01-2015 to MAY-30-2015. All complaints were related to packaging defects for the 250 mg tablets of the Cherry Flavored product from lot #ABC-01234. Specifically, there were some Grape Flavored 250 mg tablets found in the Cherry Flavored 250 mg bottles. The aforementioned lot was packaged from JAN-02-2015 to JAN-07-2015 and it was distributed in the U.S. East Coast. Complaints were received from the following states: Florida, North Carolina, and New York. No other complaints were received.

After gathering information through a change analysis, is-is not matrix, cause and effects diagram, and current barrier analysis, it is suspected that one of the controls that could have avoided the product mix-up is an effective line clearance. As per procedure ABC-SOP-1971 (Rev. 12), all the line operators, along with the line mechanics must perform the line clearance at the end of each lot. Once finished, the QA Technician must approve the line clearance.

In the current situation, the lot was completed just 15 minutes before the end of the shift. In normal situations, when the production is continuous, the next shift would complete the line clearance before starting the new lot. However, after Lot #ABC-01234 was completed, a one-week vacation period started and the line clearance was not performed. The procedure does not cover this situation when there has been some prolonged period between the end of one lot and the beginning of the next lot. Also, the batch record reviewer did not notice that the space for line clearance for Lot #ABC-01234 was completed as "N/A." He mentioned that while reviewing the batch records he was also auditing other non-related records (multitasking).

In order to avoid the reoccurrence and/or occurrence of the root causes, the following actions were taken:

a. Revise procedure ABC-1971 "Startup of Production for Same-Dosage Product" to include instructions to verify line clearance performed by previous shift.

b. Revise procedure ABC-1972 "Startup of Production for Different-Dosage Product" to include instructions to verify line clearance performed by previous shift.

c. Revise procedure ABC-1999 "Batch record review" to establish that the reviewer cannot be performing any other task while reviewing the batch record.

These actions will be evaluated three months after their implementation in order to determine if the root causes have been eliminated.

PROBLEM DESCRIPTION

Company ABC's Customer Service Center received 99 complaints from MAY-01-2015 to MAY-30-2015. All complaints were related to packaging defects for the 250 mg tablets of the Cherry Flavored product from lot #ABC-01234. Specifically, there were some Grape Flavored 250 mg tablets found in the Cherry Flavored 250 mg bottles. The aforementioned lot was packaged from JAN-02-2015 to JAN-07-2015 and it was distributed in the U.S. East Coast. Complaints were received from the following states: Florida, North Carolina, and New York. No other complaints were received.

IMMEDIATE ACTION(S) TAKEN

Following procedure ABC-1934 (rev. 7), a 20% of the reserve sample bottles for lot #ABC-01234 were verified randomly to determine if the defect was present on the reserve samples. Only one bottle was found with Cherry Flavored 250 mg mixed with Grape Flavored 250 mg. Also, a 20% of the reserve samples of lots #ABC-01232, #ABC-01233, #ABC-01235 and #ABC-01236 were verified randomly. In none of these other lots the defects were observed.

Lots #ABC-01232 and #ABC-01233 were for Grape Flavored 250 mg, while lots #ABC-01234, #ABC-01235, and #ABC-01236 were for Cherry Flavored 250 mg. All these lots (from #ABC-01232 to #ABC-01236 were packed in Line #1.

INITIAL IMPACT ASSESSMENT

The Failure Mode and Effects Analysis (FMEA) for packaging lines was analyzed (see attached FMEA-PACK-001, Rev. 011015). Based on the FMEA, the mix-up of products has various risk levels. For the potential failure mode of product mix-up with different flavor of the same product with the same dosage, the risk is ranked as medium. In this case, an investigation with root cause analysis must be performed and completed within 30 calendar days.

Following procedure ABC-1934 (rev. 7) after receiving two mix-up complaints for the same lot, the 20% of the reserve sample bottles for lot #ABC-01234 were verified randomly to determine if the defect was present on the reserve samples, resulting in only one bottle found with Cherry Flavored 250 mg mixed with Grape Flavored 250 mg. Also, 20% of the reserve samples of lots #ABC-01232, #ABC-01233, #ABC-01235, and #ABC-01236 were verified randomly. In none of these four lots the defects were observed. So, the product mix-up failure seems to be related only to lot #ABC-1234. This lot consists of 100,000 bottles. The 99 defective bottles of the customer complaints represent 0.099% of the lot.

Risk of the event: ☐ Negligible/Low ■ Medium ☐ High

INVESTIGATION DETAILS

a. Overview:

Company ABC manufactures chewable tablets to treat headaches in six different presentations: Cherry Flavored 250 mg, Grape Flavored 250 mg, Lemon Flavored 250 mg, Cherry Flavored 500 mg, Grape Flavored 500 mg, and Lemon Flavored 500 mg. There are five non-dedicated packaging lines; that is, any line can handle any one of the six presentations. The product is distributed in the U.S. East Coast.

The plant operates on three shifts. The first shift currently has the most senior employees, while the third shift has the most recent employees. The new employees are on a "learning curve" during their first three months working directly with the first-shift operators. After that period, they start to work on their shift, without any direct input from their trainers. Company ABC experienced a massive hiring of employees during the period of FEB-01-2015 to MAY-31-2015.

The company has been receiving customer complaints since MAY-01-2015 due to product mix up on lot #ABC-01234. In Florida, 25 complaints were received for the Cherry Flavored 250 mg mixed with Grape Flavored 250 mg. In North Carolina, there were 26 customer complaints for the Cherry Flavored 250 mg mixed with Grape Flavored 250 mg. In New York, 48 complaints were received for the Cherry Flavored 250 mg mixed with Grape Flavored 250 mg.

b. Change Analysis:

A change analysis was developed as part of the investigation. The key question to answer in this part of the investigation is: Has something changed in the process recently? Based on the facts gathered as part of the investigation, one of the changes was that new personnel started working on the third shift on MAY-01-2015, the date when the customer complaints started. They were hired on FEB-01-2015 and were trained on the first shift until APR-30-2015. However, tracing the packaging date of lot #ABC-01234, it was packed from JAN-02-2015 to JAN-07-2015, way before the new personnel was hired. So, the possibility that the failure is related to the new personnel is discarded.

Lot #ABC-01234 was packed from JAN-02-2015 to JAN-07-2015. This represents a change from other similar lots because the lot was packaged right after returning from a one-week holiday vacation period. This situation will be analyzed further during the investigation, to determine if the time frame when the lot was packaged has a relationship with the defects.

c. Comparison Matrix (Is-Is Not):

A Comparison Matrix (Is-Is Not Analysis) was also performed as part of the investigation. The purpose is to identify why the failure occurs under certain conditions, but not under other conditions. Once the difference is analyzed, probable root causes can be identified. The results of this analysis are presented here:

		Is Describe the problem in detail	**Is Not** Describe what the problem could be (reasonably), but IS NOT
What	Which object (process, product or system) has the problem?	Cherry Flavored 250 mg	Cherry Flavored (500 mg), Grape Flavored (250 and 500 mg), and Lemon Flavored (250 and 500 mg) dosages.
	What is exactly the problem?	Packaging process defects (product mix up)	Manufacturing process defects.
Where	Where is the problem located geographically?	Florida, North Carolina, New York	Other states in the United States' East Coast
	Where is the problem located within the object (process, product or system)?	Packaging process	Manufacturing process
When	When (time, day, month, year) was the first time the problem was observed or detected?	Customer complaints received since MAY-01-2015	Before MAY-01-2015
	When, since the first time, the problem has been observed again? Any trend can be observed?	Only for lot #ABC-01234. The lot was packaged from JAN-02-2015 to JAN-07-2015	Lots before or after lot #ABC-01234
	When, in the object's lifecycle (product, process or system) was the problem observed for the first time?	The product has been manufactured since JAN-10-2010. However, only complaint was received since MAY-01-2015.	Before MAY-01-2015

(Continued)

(Continued)

How Much	How many objects (product, process or systems) have the same problem?	99 customer complaints of Lot #ABC-01234	No complaints for other lots
	How many defects are in every object (product, process or system)?	Only one defect (Cherry Flavored 250 mg mixed with Grape Flavored 250 mg)	No other defects
	Can any trend be observed?	No trends have been observed after MAY-01-2015	No trends have been observed before MAY-01-2015

From the matrix presented above, following are some of the questions that will be considered as part of the analysis for the investigation:

- Why is the failure occurring only in the Cherry Flavored 250 mg, but not in the other presentations?
- Why is the failure occurring in the packaging process, but not in the manufacturing process?
- Why is the failure occurring only in Florida, North Carolina, and New York, but not in any other states of the East Coast?
- Why is the failure occurring only for lot #ABC-01234, but not for the lots packaged before or after it?

d. Cause and Effect Diagram (Fishbone):

A cause and effect diagram was developed as part of the investigation. The purpose of the fishbone is to identify probable root causes that can be associated to an effect. This cause-and-effect relationship needs to be proved with further investigation. The cause and effect diagram for the product mix-up failure is presented here:

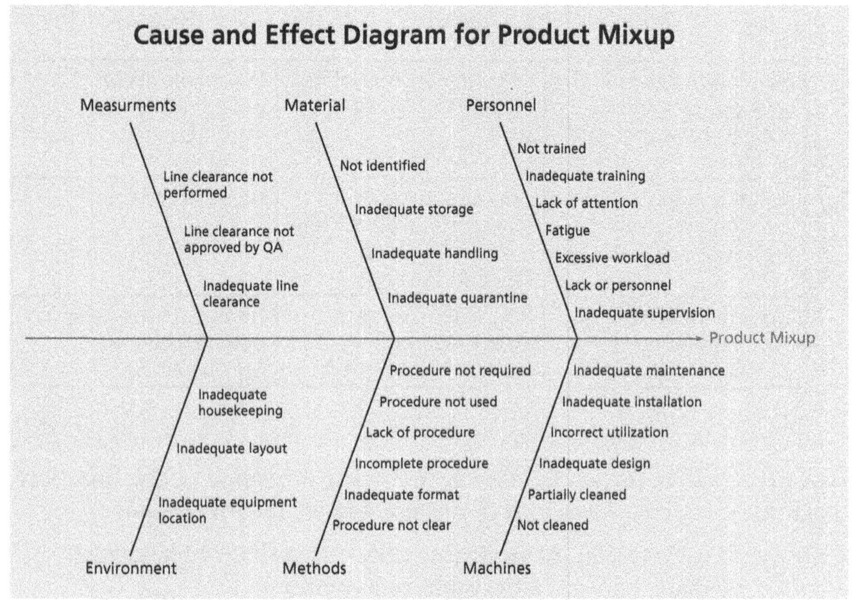

e. Current Barrier (Controls) Analysis

A current barrier (controls) analysis was performed in order to evaluate the current controls available in the process to detect or prevent the failure. The basic question is: Was there any control in place to prevent or detect the failure? If the answer is Yes, then we need to ask why it did not work. If the Answer is No, then we will probably have a "lack of control" root cause.

For the current investigation, the defects were found by the customer. So, that means none of the current controls were able to find the defects. Then, an analysis of why did the controls not worked must be performed.

CONCLUSION ABOUT ROOT CAUSE(S)

What is (are) the probable root cause(s) of this event?

After gathering information through a change analysis, is-is not matrix, cause and effects diagram, and current barrier analysis, it is suspected that one of the controls that could have avoided the product mix-up is an effective line clearance. As per procedure ABC-SOP-1971 (Rev. 12) *Startup of Production for Same-Dosage Product,* all the line operators, along with the line mechanics must perform the line clearance at the end of each lot. Once finished, the QA technician must approve the line clearance.

Looking at the batch record for lot #ABC-01233 of Grape Flavored 250 mg (the lot packaged right before lot #ABC-01234), it was noticed that lot #ABC-01233 was finished on DEC-26-2014 at 10:45 p.m., just 15 minutes before the end of the shift. There is no evidence that the machine was adequately cleaned and that all remaining material was removed from the area. The space where the cleaning is documented appeared as "N/A" (not applicable). When the line operators and mechanics were interviewed, they mentioned that "N/A" was documented because they did not complete the line clearance by the end of the shift and they assumed that when production restarted the new shift would perform and document the line clearance, as it usually happens when the lot is finished during the shift.

On JAN-02-2015, when production restarted after the one-week vacation period, lot #ABC-01234 started at 07:25 a.m. (the shift starts at 07:00 a.m.). However, there is no evidence that any line clearance was performed prior to the start of the batch. When the line operators and mechanics were interviewed, they mentioned that procedure ABC-SOP-1971 (Rev. 12) requires the line clearance at the end of the lot, not at the beginning of the new lot. They also mentioned that they always rely on the line clearance performed by the previous shift.

When the batch record reviewer was interviewed about why he did not notice the "N/A" entry on the line clearance space, he mentioned that while reviewing the batch records he was also auditing other non-related records (multi-tasking).

Based on these observations, the following were identified as contributors to the mix-up incident:

- **Line clearance not performed (causal factor):**
  - It is noticed that not performing the line clearance was the direct situation that caused the product mix-up. The line clearance is the main control to avoid mix-ups.
- **Incomplete procedure (root cause):**
  - Procedure ABC-SOP-1971 (Rev. 12) *Startup of Production for Same-Dosage Product,* establishes that all the line operators, along with the line mechanics must perform the line clearance at the end of each lot. Once finished, the QA technician must approve the line clearance. In the current situation, the lot was completed just 15 minutes before the end of the shift. In normal situations, when the production is continuous, the next shift would complete the line clearance before starting the new lot. However, after Lot #ABC-01234 was completed, a one-week vacation period started and the line clearance was not

performed. The procedure does not cover this situation when there has been some prolonged period between the end of one lot and the beginning of the next lot.

- **Lack of attention (root cause):**
  - The batch record reviewer did not notice that the space for line clearance for Lot #ABC-01234 was completed as "N/A." He mentioned that while reviewing the batch records he was also auditing other non-related records (multitasking).

FINAL DISPOSITION

After completing the investigation process, it was determined to monitor, during the next three months, the customer complaints for Lot #ABC-01234 and subsequent lots. If no other customer complaints due to product mix-up on this or subsequent lots are received during these three months, the investigation will be closed. Otherwise, the investigation will be expanded.

CF or RC	Description	CO CA PA	Action	Responsible	Due date	Metrics
CF	Line clearance not performed	CO	Awareness to all packaging personnel	J. Smith	JUN-15-2015	All packaging personnel are briefed on the failure and its regulatory consequences
RC	Incomplete procedure	CA	Revise procedure ABC-1971 (rev. 12) *Startup of Production for Same-Dosage Product* to include instructions to verify line clearance performed by previous shift	M. Pena	JUL-30-2015	Three months after the implementation of the revised procedure, evaluate that no mix-up due to inadequate line clearance has occurred

(Continued)

(Continued)

RC	Incomplete procedure	PA	Revise procedure ABC-1972 (rev.16) *Startup of Production for Different-Dosage* Product to include instructions to verify line clearance performed by previous shift	M. Pena	JUL-30-2015	Three months after the implementation of the revised procedure, evaluate that no mix-up due to inadequate line clearance has occurred
RC	Lack of attention	CA	Revise procedure ABC-1999 (rev. 23) *Batch record review* to establish that the reviewer cannot be performing any other task while reviewing the batch record	J. Doe	JUL-30-2015	Three months after the implementation of the revised procedure, evaluate that no batch record documentation error has been missed

Legend:

CF = causal factor

RC = root cause

CO = correction

CA = corrective action

PA = preventive action

8.6 CAPA PLAN EXAMPLES

This chapter discusses real examples of CAPA plans. Only applicable sections of each case are presented.

Example 1

Situation/Root causes

Company X, a manufacturer of portable medical devices that operate with a rechargeable battery identified a significant increase in the number of complaints due to short battery life. The supplier's investigation determined that the reduced life was the result of a defective raw material used in two different lots of batteries.

Correction

a. Hold the distribution of portable devices containing defective batteries.

b. Rework inventory of portable devices containing defective batteries.

c. Sent replacement batteries to customers of all products using the defective batteries.

Corrective action

a. The supplier created a plan to enhance the incoming testing of components as well as its in-process and final release testing of rechargeable batteries, including a specific test to detect the cause of this situation.

b. The supplier will provide monthly reports over the next six months to verify that its inspection program was adequate to identify nonconforming raw materials and finished batteries before they were shipped to Company X.

c. An incoming test able to detect this specific problem with rechargeable batteries was implemented. The next five lots of batteries received from supplier will be tested using a tightened sampling plan. After that, a normal sampling plan will be established to test every lot of rechargeable batteries received.

d. Perform a comprehensive audit to the supplier of rechargeable batteries.

Effectiveness verification

a. The Quality Department established a report to monitor complaints received due to decreased battery life during the next 12 months. This report will be used to verify that corrective actions were effective.

Preventive action

a. The Purchasing Department will perform a risk-based assessment of all purchased materials to classify each material/item and their potential failure mode.

Example 2

Situation/Root causes

After a surge in complaints due to under-filled tablet bottles, it was discovered that several metallic pins in the filler machine #3 were bent. Maintenance procedures and instructions for this filler machine #3 did not include the verification of the pins as part of the periodic maintenance activities.

Correction

All pins in the filler machine #3 were inspected and those found to be bent were changed.

Corrective action

Include the periodic inspection of pins as part of the preventive maintenance of tablet filler machine #3.

Effectiveness verification

a. Monitor for correct number of tablets 30 lots filled during the next two months. A statistically-appropriate sampling plan must be used. Corrective action will be considered effective if no under-filled bottles are detected.

b. Monitor customer complaints due to under-filled bottles for a period of three months after implementation of the corrective action. Corrective action will be considered effective if no complaints are received due to under-filled bottles.

Preventive action

Include the periodic inspection of pins as part of the preventive maintenance of the other three filler machine operating in this site (tablet filler machine #1, #2, and #4).

Effectiveness verification

Monitor customer complaints due to under-filled bottles (three months after implementation of the preventive action). The preventive action will be effective if no complaints are received due to under-filled bottles.

Example 3

Situation/Root causes
During an audit of the aseptic filling suite, several workers were observed inside the aseptic filling room exhibiting inappropriate aseptic conduct such as rapid movement throughout the class 100 area.

Correction
A meeting was held with all filling operators to reinforce adequate aseptic behavior necessary when working inside the class 100 area.

Corrective action
Revise SOP 123 to include clear instructions on personnel movements in the class 100 filling rooms.

Interim action
While SOP 123 new version becomes effective, proper movement techniques will be discussed at the beginning of each shift by group/leader/supervisory personnel. Random audits will be performed by supervisors during each shift.

Effectiveness verification
During the next three months, a competence assessment/performance assessment of a sample of personnel working in rooms X, Y and Z will be performed. The sample must include personnel from all shifts. The assessment will be performed by supervisory personnel using a checklist developed from aseptic instructions included in the new version of the SOP 123. The corrective action will be considered effective if all evaluated filling operators exhibit appropriate aseptic techniques.

Example 4

Situation/Root causes
Sales representative for a manufacturer of surgical sutures suggested to improve labeling of the individual suture packets to avoid the selection of incorrect sizes. Currently only written (numerical) description of the size is provided on labeling. Providing more than one visual indicator of size will optimize usability of the product. A survey was performed among some key customers to assess their preference.

Correction
Design a plan to phase out existing packaging configuration for affected product codes.

Preventive action
A color coded labeling system was implemented for the primary and secondary packaging containers. In addition to the color indicator, a repetitive pattern displaying the diameter size (in number) will cover both size of the surface of the primary packaging container. The same color-coded scheme and repetitive printing model was applied to other five company's products. A communication campaign will be devised to inform customers of the changes in labeling.

Effectiveness verification
Three months after the initial distribution of new packaging, perform a survey among a statistical sample of customers to verify their acceptability of the new labeling. The action will be considered effective if at least 60% of the surveyed customers prefer the new labeling.

Example 5

The following example describe a frequent situation where no root causes are identified and the only action performed is a "retraining." Even this is not a desirable situation, we can demonstrate with this example that an "elegant" effectiveness verification can be accomplished.

Corrective action
Discuss the investigation with the manufacturing operators, mechanics and QA personnel emphasizing the importance to properly set table presses, document mechanical interventions, and so on as established in procedure 123 rev. F.

Effectiveness verification

a. Using a checklist created to assess the elements discussed, perform a random verification of compression works (ten batches each shift) during the next two months. This action will be considered effective if all operators were following proper instructions.

b. No deviations generated during the next three months due to deviations to procedure 123, rev. F.

8.7 FINAL RECOMMENDATIONS

Table 8.8 Final investigations and CAPA recommendations.

Topics	Recommendations
Problem detection	• Use risk assessment criteria to prioritize your investigation and CAPA activities • Monitor in-conformance results • Consider all available sources of CAPA data
Problem investigation	• Do not use human error as root cause • Establish the requirements for using problem-solving tools (comparison diagram, timeline, fishbone, FTA, and so on).
Human error investigation	• Interview human beings involved with each incident • Investigate human factors • Look for precursor (latent) factors
CAPA Plan	• At least one corrective action per each root cause • Do not use *evaluate*, *analyze*, or *assess* as corrective or preventive action • Do not overuse retraining
Effectiveness evaluation	• Do not use a fixed period of time • Link it to root cause, not symptoms
Management of the CAPA system	• Maintain only one CAPA system • Correlate systems, if using more than one (external, internal, and so on) • Develop your investigation/CAPA personnel
Documenting Investigations/CAPA	• Clarity • Readability • Economy • Correctness
Training for Investigations/CAPA	• Certify your investigation and CAPA personnel • Evaluate the effectiveness of your investigation and CAPA training

(Continued)

(Continued)

Table 8.8 Final investigations and CAPA recommendations.

Human error prevention	• Eliminate the error source; make the error impossible by design • Do not allow personnel to operate by memory (read, execute, and document is the best recipe to prevent human errors) • Reduce the error opportunity using physical barriers • Mitigate the consequences of an error • Make the errors detectable before they create a greater problem • Reinforce supervision for new employees, tasks, or equipment) • Improve documents/work instructions: • Employees without supervision must follow the procedures • Provide reminders (warnings) when appropriate • Improve the effectiveness of the training

Appendix A

ADDITIONAL RESOURCES

Andersen, B. and T. Fagerhaug. 2006. *Root Cause Analysis: Simplified Tools and Techniques*. 2nd ed. Milwaukee, WI: ASQ Quality Press.

Gawande, A. 2010. *The Checklist Manifesto: How to Get Things Right*. New York, NY: Metropolitan Books.

Phillips, J. J. and R. D. Stone. 2002. *How to Measure Training Results: A Practical Guide to Tracking the Six Key Indicators*. New York, NY: McGraw-Hill.

Reason, J. and A. Hobbs. 2003. *Managing Maintenance Error: A Practical Guide*. Burlington, VT: Ashgate.

Rodríguez-Pérez, J. 2014. *The FDA and Worldwide Current Good Manufacturing Practices and Quality System Requirements Guidebook for Finished Pharmaceuticals*. Milwaukee, WI: ASQ Quality Press.

Rodríguez-Pérez, J., and Manuel Peña-Rodríguez. 2012. "Fail-Safe FMEA." *Quality Progress*, January, 31–36.

Wilson, P. F., L. D. Dell, and G. F. Anderson. 1993. *Root Cause Analysis: A Tool for Total Quality Management*. Milwaukee, WI: ASQ Quality Press.

USEFUL WEB SITES

http://ec.europa.eu/enterprise/sectors/pharmaceuticals/documents/eudralex/index_en.htm

The body of European Union legislation in the pharmaceutical sector is compiled here.

http://www.asq.org

The American Society for Quality (ASQ) is the world's leading membership organization devoted to quality. This site provides useful information, resources, and links for quality topics.

http://www.fda.gov

This is the entry page to the U.S. Food and Drug Administration.

http://www.fda.gov/ora

This page contains significant ORA documents (consent decrees, 483 forms, Establishment Inspection Reports, and many more regulatory documents) under its ORA FOIA Electronic Reading Room.

http://www.fda.gov/iceci/enforcementActions/Warningletters/default.htm

This is the place to see FDA published warning letters sent to regulated firms.

http://www.fda.gov/Safety/Recalls/default.htm

This section includes the most significant product actions over the last five years based on the extent of distribution and the degree of health risk. In this section, you will find a listing of FDA and industry press releases regarding product recalls. It includes a link to weekly FDA Enforcement Reports.

http://www.capapr.com

Author's web page devoted to the CAPA system and the regulated industry.

http://www.calidadpr.com

Author's page devoted to general quality topics (in Spanish).

http://www.ich.org

The International Conference on Harmonization of Technical Requirements for Registration of Pharmaceuticals for Human Use (ICH) is a unique project that brings together the regulatory authorities of Europe, Japan, and the United States and experts from the pharmaceutical industry in the three regions to discuss scientific and technical aspects of product registration.

http://www.imdrf.org

The International Medical Device Regulators Forum (IMDRF) was conceived in February 2011 as a forum to discuss future directions in medical device regulatory harmonization. It is a voluntary group of medical device regulators from around the world who have come together to build on the strong foundational work of the Global Harmonization Task Force on Medical Devices (GHTF), and to accelerate international medical device regulatory harmonization and convergence.

Acronyms

CAPA	Corrective and preventive action
CDER	FDA's Center for Drug Evaluation and Research
CDRH	FDA's Center for Devices and Radiological Health
CFR	U.S. Code of Federal Regulations
CGMP	Current good manufacturing practice
EU	European Union
FAR	Field alert report
FDA	U.S. Food and Drug Administration
FMEA	Failure modes and effects analysis
FTA	Fault tree analysis
GHTF	Global Harmonization Task Force
HACCP	Hazard analysis and critical control point
ICH	International Conference on Harmonization
IMDRF	International medical device regulators forum
ISO	International Standardization Organization
MDR	Medical device reporting
NCR	Nonconformance report
OOC	Out-of-control
OOS	Out-of-specification
OOT	Out-of-trend
ORA	FDA's Office of Regulatory Affairs
QC	Quality control
QCU	Quality control unit
QMS	Quality management system

QSIT	FDA's quality system inspection technique
QSR	FDA's quality system regulations
RCA	Root cause analysis
SPC	Statistical process control

Glossary

adverse trend: A general drift or tendency in a set of data to exceed established limits over an established period of time.

action threshold: A statistical limit based on historical data used to indicate an adverse trend, requiring an action. See OOC.

annual product review: An evaluation, conducted at least annually, that assesses the quality standards of each drug product to determine the need for changes in the drug product specifications or manufacturing or control procedures.

CAPA (corrective and preventive action): A systematic approach that includes actions needed to correct ("correction"), avoid recurrence ("corrective action"), and eliminate the cause of potential nonconforming product and other quality problems (preventive action).

CAPA plan: Encompasses the identification of corrective and/or preventive actions, their verification and/or validation (prior to implementation), their implementation, and finally the evaluation of the plan's effectiveness.

causal factor: Any failure (human, equipment, or material/component) that directly caused the incident, allowed it to occur, or allowed the consequence to be worse.

concession: A special approval granted to release a nonconforming product for use or delivery. Concessions are usually limited by time and quantity and tend to specify that nonconforming characteristics may not violate specified limits.

continuous improvement: Ongoing activities to evaluate and positively change products, processes, and the quality system to increase effectiveness.

control limit (CL): A horizontal line on a control chart that represents a boundary for a process. If the process strays beyond a control limit, it may be out of control.

correction: Action to eliminate a detected nonconformity. Corrections typically are one-time fixes. A correction is an immediate solution such as repair or rework. Also known as remedial or containment action.

corrective action: Action to eliminate the causes of a detected nonconformity or other undesirable situation. The corrective action should eliminate the recurrence of the cause.

customer: A person or organization (internal or external) that receives a product or service anywhere along the product's life cycle.

discrepancy: Datum or result outside of the expected range; an unfulfilled requirement. May be called nonconformity, defect, deviation, out of specification, out of limit, out of trend.

effectiveness: The degree to which a planned effect is achieved. Planned activities are effective if these activities are realized. Similarly, planned results are effective if these results are actually achieved. For example, an effective process is one that realizes planned activities and achieves planned results. Similarly, an effective set of characteristics or specifications is one that has the potential to realize planned activities and achieve planned results.

effectiveness evaluation: Documented process to establish that an action was effective and accomplished the objective that was intended.

efficiency: A relationship between results achieved (outputs) and resources used (inputs). Efficiency can be enhanced by achieving more with the same or fewer resources. The efficiency of a process or system can be enhanced by achieving more or getting better results (outputs) with the same or fewer resources (inputs).

current good manufacturing practices (CGMP): A set of current regulations for the control and management of manufacturing and quality control of foods, pharmaceutical products, and medical devices. GMPs are guidelines that outline the aspects of production that would affect the quality of a product. Many countries have created their own GMP guidelines that correspond with their legislation.

harm: Damage to health, including damage that can occur from the loss of product quality or availability (ICH Q9). Physical injury or damage to health of people or damage to property or the environment (ANSI/AAMI/ISO 14971:2007, ISO/IEC Guide 51:1999).

investigation: Thorough, timely, unbiased, well-documented, and scientifically sound process used to discover the root causes of the problem.

metric: A quantitative measurement that is collected, recorded, and analyzed to determine whether quality system goals and objectives have been met or exceeded or failed to meet the requirements.

monitor: To observe and check over a period of time; to maintain regular close observation over a process.

nonconformance: Non-fulfillment of specified requirements.

nonconformity: A deficiency in a characteristic, product specification, process parameter, record, or procedure that renders the quality of a product unacceptable, indeterminate, or not according to specified requirements.

objective evidence: Data that show or prove that something exists or is true. Objective evidence can be collected by means of observations, measurements, tests, or any other suitable method.

out-of-control (OOC): Any data points outside of control chart limits that represent the natural boundaries of the process.

out-of-specification (OOS): Test results (in-process and final) that fall outside the established specifications or acceptance criteria.

preventive action: Action to eliminate the cause of a potential nonconformity or other undesirable potential situation. The preventive action should prevent the occurrence of the potential cause.

product/service: The intended results of activities or processes; products/services can be tangible or intangible.

quality: The degree to which a set of inherent characteristics fulfills requirements. A measure of a product's or service's ability to satisfy the customer's stated or implied needs.

quality assurance: Proactive and retrospective activities that provide confidence that requirements are fulfilled.

quality control: The steps taken during the generation of a product or service to ensure that it meets requirements and that the product or service is reproducible.

quality management: Coordinated activities to direct and control an organization with regard to quality.

quality management system (QMS): Management system to direct and control an organization with regard to quality.

quality objectives: Specific measurable activities or processes to meet the intentions and directions as defined in the quality policy.

quality plan: The documented result of quality planning that is disseminated to all relevant levels of the organization.

quality planning: A management activity that sets quality objectives and defines the operational and/or quality system processes and the resources needed to fulfill the objectives.

quality policy: A statement of intentions and direction issued by the highest level of the organization related to satisfying customer needs. It is similar to a strategic direction that communicates quality expectations that the organization is striving to achieve.

quality system: Formalized business practices that define management responsibilities for organizational structure, processes, procedures, and resources needed to fulfill product/service requirements, customer satisfaction, and continuous improvement.

quality system regulations (QSR): U.S. medical devices regulations (Title 21 CFR §820).

requirement: Need or expectation that is stated, generally implied or obligatory.

rework: Action taken on a nonconforming product so that it will fulfill the specified requirements before it is released for distribution.

risk: The combination of the probability of occurrence of harm and the severity of that harm.

risk assessment: A systematic process for organizing information to support a risk decision that is made within a risk management process. The process consists of the identification of hazards and the analysis and evaluation of risks associated with exposure to those hazards.

risk management: The systematic application of quality management policies, procedures, and practices to the tasks of assessing, controlling, communicating, and reviewing risk.

root cause: A gap in a process input or supporting business system that is, at least partly, responsible for the incident. It is the basic reason why causal factors occur and/or persist.

root cause analysis (RCA): Analysis necessary to determine the original or true cause of a system, product, or process nonconformity. This effort extends beyond the effects of a problem to discover its most fundamental cause.

specification: Any requirement with which a product, process, service, or other activity must conform.

stakeholder: An individual or organization having an ownership or interest in the delivery, results, and metrics of the quality system framework or business process improvements.

trend: A sequence or pattern of data. Analysis of a trend is performed to detect a special cause amidst the random variation of data.

timeliness: A time frame commensurate with the risk and magnitude of the issue; considered reasonable by a company that is concerned with protecting the public health.

validation: Confirmation, through the provision of objective evidence, that the requirements for a specific intended use or application can be consistently fulfilled.

verification: Confirmation, through the provision of objective evidence, that specified requirements have been fulfilled.

Bibliography

Ammerman, M. 1998. *The Root Cause Analysis Handbook: A Simplified Approach to Identifying, Correcting, and Reporting Workplace Errors.* New York: Productivity Press.

Arter, D. 2015. "Separate Steps. Mixing Corrective and Preventive Actions Results in Ineffective Use." *Quality Progress,* January, 38–43.

Bridges, W. and R. Tew. 2010. "Human Factors Missing from Process Safety Management, *6th Global Congress on Process Safety,* San Antonio.

Center for Chemical Process Safety 2007. *Human Factors Methods for Improving Performance in the Process Industries.* New Jersey: Wiley-Interscience.

Daniel, A. and E. Kimmelman. 2008. *The FDA and Worldwide Quality System Regulations Guidebook for Medical Devices.* 2nd ed. Milwaukee, WI: ASQ Quality Press.

Dekker, S. 2006. *The Field Guide to Understanding Human Error.* Burlington, VT: Ashgate.

European Pharmaceutical GMP. *EudraLex* Volume 4 (2003). The body of European Union legislation in the pharmaceutical sector is compiled in Volume 1 and Volume 5 of the publication "The rules governing medicinal products in the European Union." It can be downloaded from: http://ec.europa.eu/enterprise/sectors/pharmaceuticals/documents/eudralex/index_en.htm.

FDA. *21 Code of Federal Regulations §Part 210: Current manufacturing practice in manufacturing, processing, packing, or holding of drugs; general* (1978). Can be downloaded from: http://www.ecfr.gov.

FDA. 21 *Code of Federal Regulations §Part 211: Current manufacturing practice for finished pharmaceuticals* (1978). Can be downloaded from: http://www.ecfr.gov

Preamble of finished pharmaceuticals can be downloaded from: http://www.fda.gov/downloads/AboutFDA/CentersOffices/CDER/UCM095852.txt.

FDA. 21 *Code of Federal Regulation §Part 820: Medical Devices: Current Good Manufacturing Practice (CGMP) Final Rule: Quality System Regulations* (1996). Can be downloaded from: http://www.ecf.gov.

Preamble of Medical Device Quality System Regulations can be downloaded from http://www.fda.gov/downloads/MedicalDevices/DeviceRegulationandGuidance/PostmarketRequirements/QualitySystems Regulations/MedicalDeviceQualitySystemsManual/UCM122806.pdf.

FDA. *Guide to Inspections of Quality Systems* (1999). This guide can be downloaded from: www.fda.gov/downloads/ICECI/Inspections/UCM142981.pdf.

FDA. *Guidance for Industry. Investigating Out-of-Specification (OOS)* Test Results for Pharmaceutical Production (2006).

Note: All FDA guidances can be downloaded from: http://www.fda.gov/regulatoryinformation/guidances/default.htm.

FDA. *Guidance Do It By Design—An Introduction to Human Factors in Medical Devices* (1996).

FDA. *General Principles of Software Validation: Final Guidance for Industry and FDA Staff* (2002).

FDA. *Guidance for Industry: Quality Systems Approach to Pharmaceutical Current Good Manufacturing Practice Regulations* (2006).

FDA. *Guidance for Industry Sterile Drug Products Produced by Aseptic Processing—Current Good Manufacturing Practice* (2004).

FDA. *Guidance for Industry: ICH Q10 Pharmaceutical Quality System.* (2009).

Global Harmonization Task Force. SG 3 (PD)/N18R8: Quality management system—Medical Devices—Guidance on corrective action and preventive action and related QMS processes (2009). This guidance can be downloaded from: http://www.ghtf.org/sg3/sg3-proposed.html.

International Standard, ISO 9001:2015 *Quality management systems—Requirements.*

International Standard, ISO 13485:2003 Medical devices—*Quality management systems— Requirements for regulatory purposes.*

International Standard, ISO/TR 14969: 2004 *Medical devices—Quality management systems—Guidance on the application of ISO 13485:2003.*

Keller, G. 2012. *The ONE Thing: The Surprisingly Simple Truth Behind Extraordinary Results.* Austin, Tx: Rellek Publishing Partner.

Kirkpatrick, D. L. and J. D. Kirkpatrick. 2006. *Evaluating Training Programs.* 3rd ed. San Francisco, CA: Berrett-Koehler Publishers.

Kirkpatrick, D. L. and J. D. Kirkpatrick. 2007. *Implementing the Four Levels: A Practical Guide for Effective Evaluation of Training Programs.* San Francisco, CA: Berrett-Koehler Publishers.

Kohn, L. T., J. M. Corrigan, and M. S. Donaldson, eds. *To Err is Human: Building a Safer Health System.* Washington, D.C.: Institute of Medicine Committee on Quality of Health Care in America.

Okes, D. 2009. *Root Cause Analysis: The Core of Problem Solving and Corrective Action.* Milwaukee, WI: ASQ Quality Press.

Peña-Rodríguez, M. E. 2013. *Statistical Process Control for the FDA-Regulated Industry.* Milwaukee, WI: ASQ Quality Press.

Reason, J. 1990. *Human Error.* New York: Cambridge University Press.

Reason, J. 2000. *Human Error: Models and Management.* BMJ 2000;320: 768–70.

Rodríguez-Pérez, J. 2010. *CAPA for the FDA-Regulated Industry.* Milwaukee, WI: ASQ Quality Press.

Rodríguez-Pérez, J. 2012. *Quality Risk management in the FDA Regulated Industry.* Milwaukee, WI: ASQ Quality Press

Tague, N.R. 2005. *The Quality Toolbox.* 2nd ed. Milwaukee, WI: ASQ Quality Press.

Swain, A. D. and H. E. Guttman. 1983. *Handbook of Human Reliability Analysis with Emphasis on Nuclear Power Plant Applications.* NUREG/CR 1278. Albuquerque, NM: Sandia National Laboratories

Index

Page numbers in *italics* refer to figures, tables and illustrations.

A

actions not as planned, 101
actions taken, 157
active failures, 103–105
Active Implantable Medical Devices Directive 90/385 EEC (AIMD), 13, 14
activity analysis, 113–114
adequate trending, 138–139
administrative barriers, 70, *71*
adulteration of product, 51
adverse trends, 91, 144
Analyze Data for Trends, 57
annual product review (APRs), 92–94
ANOVA, 68
attention and motivation, 108–109

B

barrier control analysis, 70–71, *71*
  administrative, *71*
  examples of, *71*
  physical and natural, *71*
batch records, 98, 107, 122, 125, 129, 181, 188
bathtub curve, 137
behavior (transfer of training), 88–89
benchmarking, 122, 128
best practices, investigation of, 135
  abuse of human error and retraining, 147
  CAPA plan, 136, 139
  CAPA systems without correlation, 146
  for correcting symptoms and root causes of errors, 142
  effectiveness evaluation, 136–137
  effectiveness verification, 144–145
  errors identified but not corrected, 141
  errors not identified, 140–141
  for interim actions, 142–143
  software and CAPA system, 147–148
blaming, 130
Boolean logic, 75
brainstorming, 74
burn-in period, 137
Business Excellence Consulting Inc. (BEC), 150

C

calibration and maintenance records, 47
Canadian national standards, 30
CAPA circle, *45*
CAPA expert certification
  content of, 149–154
  elements of, *155*
  training efforts, effectiveness of, 155
CAPA forms, 161
  CAPA plan, *172*
  CAPA plan assessment, *177–179*
  human error investigation, *168–171*
  investigation report, *162–163*
  investigation report assessment, *173–176*
  root cause analysis checklist, *164–167*
CAPA management, 91, 140
CAPA plans, 8, 12, 44, 77, 80–81
  assessment form, *177–179*
  best practices, 136, 139
  content of, 159
  document, 83
  "double digit" rule, 84, 139
  effective corrective and preventive actions, 81–82
  effectiveness evaluation, 84–90, 136–137
  examples of, 189–193
  form, *172*
  implementation of, 83
  interim actions, 142–143
  stages of, 135–136
  training effectiveness, 85–90
  validation and verification prior to implementation, 82–83
  verification of, 84–85
CAPA processes
  adequate trending, lack of, 138–139
  barrier analysis, 70–71
  fixing symptoms, 64–66
  flow chart, *44*
  ICH Q9, 49

initial impact assessment, 47–56
problem description, 66–68
problem detection, 45–56
problem investigation, 59–80
process flow, *43*
process trending, 56–59
product and quality issues, 45–47
relationship among §820.90, §820.100, and §820.198, *46*
root cause categories, 77–80
root cause identification processes and tools, 72–77
symptoms, causal factors, and root causes, 60–62

CAPA recommendations, *194–195*
cause and effect diagrams. *See* Ishikawa diagram
Center for Drug Evaluation and Research (CDER), 23
change analysis, 68, *69*
change-point analysis, 68
chronology, use of, 67–68
closed loop system, 3
commission errors, 103
comparison matrix, 70
complaint handling practices, 33–35
compliance writing, 159–160
do's and don'ts for, *160*
constant failures period, 137
control charts, 47, 57–59, 68, 144
corrections, definition of, 4
corrective action, 4
corrective and preventive action system (CAPA)
best practices for, 91
concept of, 1–4
for correcting the symptom, 141–142
corrective and preventive action, 8–12, 21–22
current observations and regulatory trends, 35–37
data sources, *6*
definitions of, 4
effectiveness verification, 144–145
elements of, 8
example of, *63*
external investigation, 96
failure investigations, conduct of, 21
failure modes and effects analysis (FMEA) and, 94–96
FDA Quality Metric Program, 92–94
feeders of, *7*
history, *9–10*
interim actions, 142–143
investigation phase *versus* fixing causes, 7–8
investigation plan, 133–134
ISO 13485:2003, 31–32
management of, 90–96
manufacturing quality system and, *5*
within new version of ISO 13485, 32
nonconformance investigations, 12
preventive actions, 143–144
procedure for, 3–4
process metrics, 91–94
relation with other quality subsystems, 5
risk management, 94–96
root cause, identification of, 140–141
software, reliance on, 147–148
structure of, 90–91
timeliness, lack of, 134–137
"vicious circle" of investigation, 45
violations of, 2
without correlation, 146

current barrier analysis, 181, *186*
current good manufacturing practices (CGMP), 13, 24, 35
for medicinal products, 13
for pharmaceuticals, 14–15, 25–27
customer complaints, 2, 31, 60, 68, 85, 138, 143, 180, 188, 191
customer satisfaction, 1, 87

D

Daniel, A., 90
data analysis, 68
data integrity
characteristics of, 99
and human error, 99
data repository systems, 2
data segregation, 68
deficiencies and warning letters, 118–119
design control, 3, 17, 22, 40, 49
device master and history files, 125, 129
Do It By Design—An Introduction to Human Factors in Medical Devices, 98
document writers, 123
"double digit" rule, 84, 139

E

early failures period, 137
effectiveness evaluation, 84–90, 136–137
effectiveness verification, 144–145, 190–193
elements of certification, *155*
environmental monitoring, 58
equipment/instrument calibration system, 35

error. *See* human error
error-proof operation, design considerations for, 115
errors of commission, 103
errors of omission, 103
EudraLex, Volume 4, 13, 27–29
European pharmaceutical GMP, 27–29
execution errors, *102*
executive summary / abstract, 158
external audits and assessments, 5
external CAPA, management of, 96

F

failure modes and effects analysis (FMEA), 76, 144, 182–183
  CAPA system and, 94–96
fallibility, 130, 147
fatigue and shift work, errors caused by, 109–110
fault tree analysis (FTA), 75–76
  examples of, *76*
final disposition, 158, 180, 188
final recommendations, *194–195*
finished drugs, CGMP for, 13
fishbone diagrams, 74–75
5 *Whys* (investigative technique), 62, 74, 76
fixable root causes, 62, 76–77
flow chart, 67
Food and Drug Administration (FDA), 2
  Guidance for Industry Quality System Approach to Pharmaceutical GMP, 9, 57
  guidance on OOS test for pharmaceutical production, 23–25
  Human Factors Pre-Market Evaluation Team, 117
  medical devices QSR, 15–17, 51, 56
  out-of-specification (OOS) test, 23–25
  pharmaceutical CGMP, 14–15, 25–27
  Quality Metric Program, 92–94
  regulation for medical devices, 9
  Sterile Product Guidance, 57
food safety, 49

G

Global Harmonization Task Force (GHTF), 29
  quality management system, 33
good manufacturing practices (GMP)
  European pharmaceutical GMP, 27–29
  for medicinal products, 28
  production operations, 27
  rules and regulations governing, 27
  self-inspections, 27–28
graphical analysis tool, 68
Guttman, H. E., 103

H

hazard analysis and critical control point (HACCP), 49
histogram, 68
historical records, 19, 47
human and machine capabilities, *117*
Human Drug CGMP Notes, 134
human error, 37, 59
  abuse of, 147
  active failures, 103
  data integrity and, 99
  defined, 100
  do's and don'ts, *130*
  due to working from memory, 125
  form for investigation of, *168–171*
  groups of, 103
  and human factor, 100, 105–118
  investigation of, 119–122
  knowledge-based, 101, 102
  latent failures, 103
  meaning of, 97–99
  multitasking and, 126–127
  organizations's approach in dealing with, 118–119
  psychology and classification of, 101–105
  and retraining, 124–125, 147
  root causes related to, 122–124
  rule-based, 101, 102
  skill-based, 101
  slips and lapses of memory, 101, *102*
  statistics related to, 98–99
  steps to reduce, 127–131
  types of, *101*
  violations, 103
human factors
  compliance and quality culture, 106–108
  defined, 100
  domains of, *106*
  fatigue and shift work, 109–110
  human errors and, 100
  person-process interface, 100
  procedures and task design, 110–115
  in process operations, 116–118
  role in process performance, 105–118
  training and performance, 115–116
  workplace involvement, 108–109
human reliability engineering, 100
human reliability factors, 79, 122
human / computer interface, 116

I

ICH Q9, 40, 49
ICH Q10, 7, 14, 30
impact assessment, 47–48, 157, 182
In Vitro Diagnostic Directive 79/98 EC (IVDD), 13, 14
in-conformance data, 3
inspectional objectives, 18
interim actions, for correcting actions, 142–143
internal audits, 5, 18, 57, 129, 146
internal complaints, 47
International Association for Continuing Education and Training (IACET), 150
International Conference on Harmonization of Technical Requirements for Registration of Pharmaceuticals for Human Use (ICH), 29
International Medical Device Regulators Forum (IMDRF), 29
interview
  answering the question, 121
  characteristics of, 119–120
  ending of, 122
  initiation of, 120
  nonverbal communication, 121–122
  opening of, 120
  process of, 121
investigation plan, 72–73, 133–134, 158
investigation report
  about root causes, 180
  assessment form, *173–176*
  CAPA plan, 180
  cause and effect diagram, 185, *186*
  Comparison Matrix, *184–185*
  conclusion about root causes, 186–188
  content of, 157–158
  details of, 180, 183–186
  examples of, 179–189
  executive summary, 181–182
  final disposition, 180–181, 188–189
  form for, *162–163*
  on immediate actions taken, 182
  immediate action(s) taken, 180
  initial impact assessment, 182–183
  problem description, 179, 182
Ishikawa diagram, 74–75
Is-Is Not matrix tool, 70, 181, 186
ISO 9001:1994, 39
ISO 9001:2008, 62
ISO 9001:2015, 39–41, 86
ISO 13485:2003, 13, 30
  corrective and preventive actions, 31
  investigation and CAPA requirements, 31–32

J

job design, 114–115
job performance, 89, 110

K

Kepner, Charles T., 70
Kimmelman, E., 90
Kirkpatrick, Donald L., 87
Kirkpatrick Model for Training Effectiveness Evaluation, 87, 155
  four levels of, *87*
knowledge-based mistakes, 101–102, 125
K–T diagram, 70

L

laboratory error investigation, *66*
lack of attention, 77, 97–98, 108, 125, 129, 188
lapses of memory, *102*, 128
latent failures, 103
lawsuits, 19, 47
learning, definition of, 88
legal actions, 47
life sciences regulated industries
  CAPA regulations, 13
  complaint investigations, 33–35
  current observations and regulatory trends, 35–37
  deviations and nonconformities, 2
  European pharmaceutical GMP, 27–29
  FDA guidance, 23–27
  FDA medical devices QSR, 15–17
  FDA pharmaceutical CGMP, 14–15, 25–27
  FDA quality system inspection technique (QSIT), 17–23
  GHTF quality management system, 33
  harmonization processes, 29
  ICH Q10, 30
  investigation of anomalies, 36–37
  ISO 13485:2003, 13, 30
  non-U.S. medical device regulations, 30
  quality systems approach, 25–27
  regulatory expectations and best practices, 33–35

M

machine-human (device-user) interface, 118
manufacturing quality system, *5*
Medical Device Directive 93/42 EEC (MDD), 13, 14
medical devices, 29
  Global Harmonization Task Force (GHTF), 33
  Medical Devices QSR, 51, 56
  QMS processes, 33
  regulations, non-U.S., 14
  standardization of, 29
Medical Devices: Current Good Manufacturing Practice Final Rule: Quality System Regulations, 15
medicinal products
  CGMP for, 13
  GMP for, 28
  rules governing, 13
multitasking, 110
  and human errors, 126–127
  meaning of, 126

N

nonconformance data, 3
nonconformance investigations (NCI), 119
  types of, *56*
nonconformance report (NCR), 7–8
nonconformance (NCR) system, 35
  nonconforming product, control of, 45
non-U.S. medical devices regulations, 14
nonverbal communication, 121

O

omission errors, 103
out-of-specification (OOS) test, 48, 57
  FDA guidance on, 23–25
  full scale investigations, 24–25
  laboratory investigations, 24
  for pharmaceutical production, 23–25
out-of-trend (OOT), 57

P

Pareto analysis, 20–21
Pareto chart, 59, 92
performance shaping factors (PSFs), 100
personal performance, 77–78, 122
pharmaceutical goods manufacturing practices, 13
pharmaceutical industry, 29
pharmaceutical quality system, 28
pie charts, 20–21
poka-yoke (mistake-proofing), 127, 129
potential root causes, 12, 70, 72, 77, 82, 133, 135, 144
preventive action, 4
  best practices, 144
  CAPA systems, 143–144, 159
problem description, 66–68
problem solving, 59–60
  strategy for, 67
  trial-and-error methodology, 72
process trending
  concept of, 56–59
  tool for, 58
product defect, 105
product mixup, cause and effect diagram for, *186*
product quality review (PQRs), 28–29, 92, 94
product registration, scientific and technical aspects of, 29
product risk assessment (PRA) system, 35
production record review, 15, 35

Q

quality assurance system, 27, 36
quality audit, 16, 18–19, 46, 56, 119, 138
quality control, 28, 56
quality control unit, responsibilities of, 14
quality data, sources of, 5, *6*, 20, 46, 47
quality management system (QMS), 90
  components of, 5
  concept of, 1–4
  elements of, 3, 111
  Global Harmonization Task Force (GHTF), 33
  quality data sources, *6*
quality system inspection technique (QSIT), 17–23
quality system requirements (QSR)
  for medical devices, 13, 15–17
quality systems (QS), 26
Quality Toolbox, The (Tague), 67
query elements, 139

R

random failures period, 137
Reason, James, 101
reliability engineering, concept of, 137
risk assessment, 49–56
  criteria for, *50–51*
  example of, *54–55*
  score matrix, *53*

risk management, 144
  CAPA system and FMEA, 94–96
risk prioritization, of investigations, 55
risk-based thinking, 39–41
role play, 88
root cause analysis, 2, 59, 67
  Boolean logic and, 75
  categories of, 77–80
  cause and effect diagrams, 74–75
  checklist form, *164–167*
  elements of, *61*
  error identified but not corrected, 141
  error not identified, 140–141
  examples of, *64*
  fault tree analysis (FTA), 75–76
  5 Whys, 76
  identification processes and tools, 72–77
  identification tools, 74–75
  investigation plan, 72–73
  investigation report, 180, 186–188
  outcome of, 77
rule-based mistakes, 102
run charts, 47, 57–59

S

sabotage, 97
safety culture, 106
safety engineering, 75
sampling tables, 21–22
scatter diagram, 57, 68
sequence errors, 103
Shewhart, Walter, 59
shift scheduling, 110
short-term trending, 58
skill-based slips and lapses, 101, *102*
sleep debt, 110
sleep loss, 110
social interaction, with co-workers, 114
spare parts usage, 47
spreadsheets, 20–21
Standard Operating Procedures, 139
Startup of Production for Same-Dosage Product, 186
statistical process control (SPC), 20, 58
statistical tools, 57, 128
Sterile Product Guidance, 57
stratification of data, 68
stress management, 114
Subpart J §820.100, 16–17
Swain, A. D., 103
"Swiss cheese model" of system failure, 105
symptoms, 60
system failure, "Swiss cheese model" of, 105

T

Tague, Nancy R., 67
  Quality Toolbox, The, 67
task analysis chart, 67
task design, 112–113, *166*
  procedures and, 110–112
task saturation, 126
timelines, event, 67–68, *69*
timing errors, 103
Title 21 Code of Federal Regulations, §210 and 211, 13, 14
Title 21 Code of Federal Regulations, §820, 9, 13
training effectiveness
  CAPA plans, 85–90
  Kirkpatrick model of, 87
  steps for evaluation of, 87–90
training, for skills development, 115–116
Tregoe, Benjamin, 70
true cause-and-effect relationship, 104
true preventive actions, 95, 143–144

U

unattended root causes, 141
uncorrelated data repository systems, 2
unfavorable trends, 19
United States v Barr Laboratories, Inc. (1993), 15, 48

V

validation protocols, 22
verification of effectiveness
  adequate, 145
  best practices, 145
  inadequate, 145
  lack of, 144–145
verification protocols, 22
"vicious circle" of investigation, 45
violations, 103

W

warning letters, FDA, 118, 138
wear-out failures period, 137
Weibull distribution, 137
work redesign, 114–115
working from memory, 125
working instructions, 100, 122–123
workplace involvement, 108–109
written procedures
  deviations, 14
  role of, 111–112